DR SHLOMO BR

YOUR
DIVORCE
THERAPIST

ISBN 9780620496452

Published by

Reach Publishers, P.O.Box 1384, Wandsbeck, South Africa,

Website: www.aimtoinspire.com

E-mail: reach@webstorm.co.za

Printed by

Atlas Printers, 71 Marseilles Crescent, Briardene Industrial Park

Edited by Cathy Eberle for Reach Publishers

Cover designed by Reach Publishers
Cover image courtesy of ideago / freedigitalphotos.net

Contents

This book is dedicated to all my patients
whose troubled life touched me deeply
and inspired me to write this book for them
and for others to better their lives.

Preface

The Overview

The period pending the divorce which you are going through is probably the most turbulent period of your life. Divorce is a difficult and painful experience which puts to the test your resolve, your will and your resilience. You are bombarded with myriads of endless questions and many dilemmas. Past unresolved marital issues affect your day-to-day actions and pose a serious threat to your future way of life. Your decision-making is strongly influenced by conflicting emotions, as well as infinite advice which is not always given with good intentions. During the divorce period, you need to navigate your way through stormy and uncharted divorce waters without having any knowledge of how to do this.

This new life experience makes you feel overstressed, highly anxious, extremely unhappy and even physically sick.

If you are going through a divorce process or an interpersonal separation, then this book is written especially for you.

This book will help you manage the emotional turmoil that you experience as a result of the divorce process. This book will guide you through the divorce's emotional experiences, and will help you to find the best possible way to manage the process. The book is divided into two sections. The first section deals with the initial phase of the divorce. The second section of the book covers the different emotional divorce responses.

The first part of the book elaborates on the initial process required to make the decision to get a divorce. The divorce is a significant life-changing experience that requires careful assessment and should not be taken lightly. In this section of the book, I will help you to identify the causes of your divorce. The events and the causes that lead to your marriage dissolution will be analysed and will be based on your marital relationship. The marital interaction style, hopefully, will help you to predict future interaction with your ex-spouse, as well as helping you, in a sense, to predict the possible divorce outcomes. Furthermore, I will try to help you to shed some light on, and to identify the possible triggers underlying your divorce. Thereafter, once you are able to identify and understand the reasons leading to the end of your marriage, I will help you to try and predict the possible effects of divorce on you and your shrinking family. In addition, you will have to analyse the possible gains and losses which inevitably follow a marriage break-up. You will also, with the help of the book, have to consider additional divorce variables that can affect your future life as a divorcé/e.

The second part of the book deals with the most common emotional aspects of the divorce process. The myriad emotional reactions experienced during the divorce process will be carefully analysed. We will consider the effects of external divorce-related events, as well as the internal personal causes which, when combined, play such an important role in the multitude of divorce emotional reactions.

The external factors underlying the divorce emotional reactions are heavily dependent on whether the decision to get a divorce was taken mutually, by both spouses, or was made unilaterally, by one side only. As a general rule, in the case of a mutual decision to get a divorce, the probability to develop a severe emotional reaction will be potentially lower, facilitating a smoother divorce process, and creating a generally positive atmosphere. In such an event, there is a greater application of logical thought, and less emotionally-based decision-making. In contrast, a divorce initiated unilaterally often creates a negative atmosphere with overuse of a negative emotional tone and distorts logical thought processes.

A divorce decided upon mutually is probably the best solution for a dysfunctional relationship. A mutual decision to divorce can positively impact on the whole divorce process, and usually leads to minimal emotional disturbance in the lives of both spouses. On the other hand, a divorce unilaterally initiated within a dysfunctional relationship will be more turbulent, and causes much greater serious emotional disturbances for both spouses.

Additional external factors that can heavily influence the divorce emotional reaction include the availability of a strong support system which enhances the ability to cope with the divorce, and provides protection against developing a serious emotional reaction. Another important external factor that influences the divorce emotional reaction is the financial status. The lack of financial availability certainly does not improve the mood, while having sufficient financial resources can be helpful when coping with the divorce process.

The emotional reaction to the divorce also depends on the person's internal factors. The individual genetic makeup depends on the presence of a family history of anxiety and depression, which can facilitate the development of emotional disorders during the divorce. A positive genetic history of mood disorders can predispose both spouses to develop mood disorders. Additional internal factors that can lead to emotional disturbances include the presence of negative childhood life experiences, such as sexual or physical abuse, and the presence of neglect. Both factors represent stressful life events that can cause significant brain neuronal changes which predispose the affected spouse to develop mood disorders.

Often, the divorce initiator experiences different emotional reactions to those of the passive partner upon whom the divorce was imposed. The different divorce emotional reactions will be explained in detail in the next chapter.

My intention is to make this book as interactive as possible, instead of simply relaying information to be passively absorbed. I wish you to take part and actively complete the different tasks which will positively affect your dysfunctional emotional state.

You are required to complete the different questionnaires and the various assignments and exercises provided throughout the book. The interactive approach will increase your awareness of your specific divorce emotional reactions, and will help you to identify and understand the influence of the different factors on your emotional state. This interactive approach will foster the assimilation of new coping skills, and will improve your ability to manage your divorce emotional reactions in a more positive and constructive manner.

So thank you again for purchasing this book, dig in, and I trust that you will gain as much insight into divorce as I have.

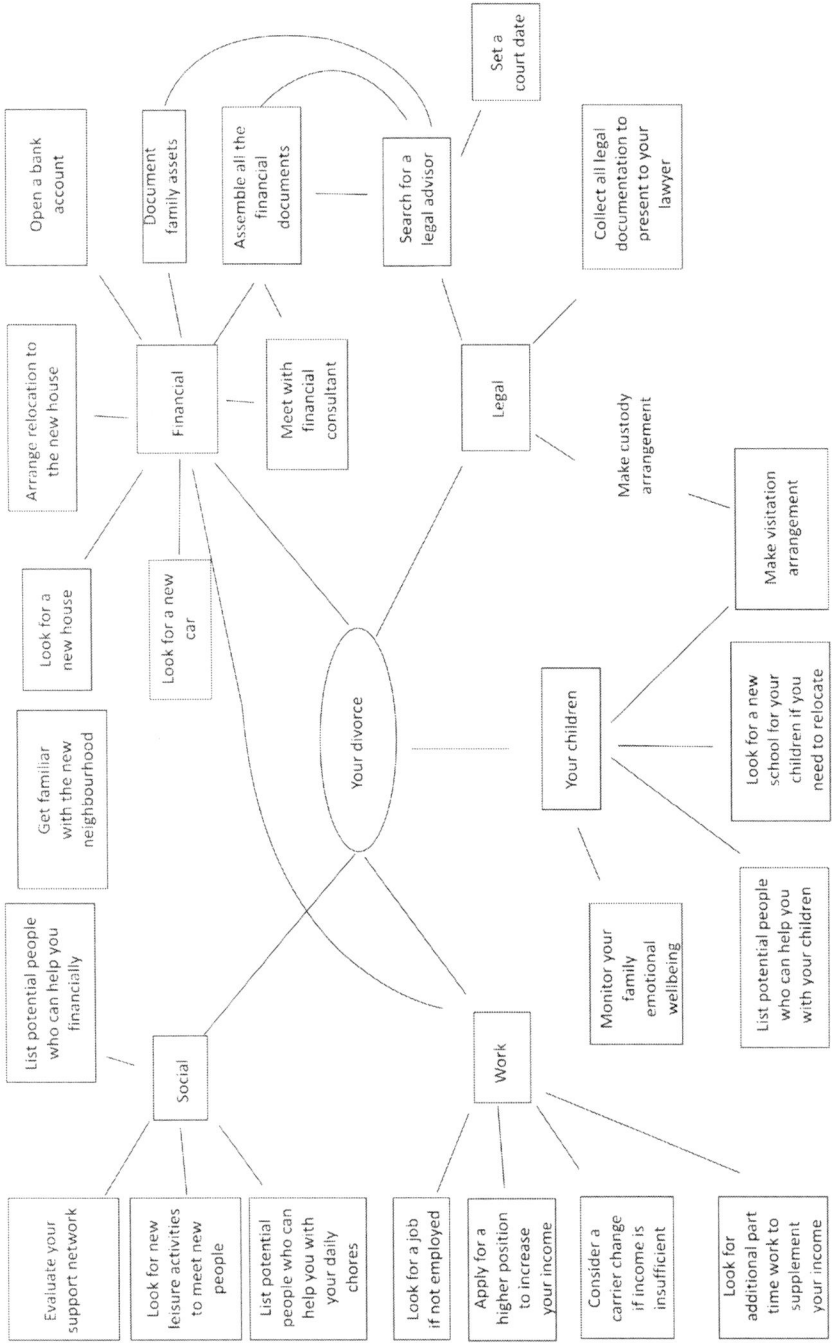

Your divorce

Financial
- Open a bank account
- Document family assets
- Assemble all the financial documents
- Meet with financial consultant
- Arrange relocation to the new house
- Look for a new house
- Look for a new car

Legal
- Search for a legal advisor
- Set a court date
- Collect all legal documentation to present to your lawyer

Your children
- Make custody arrangement
- Make visitation arrangement
- Look for a new school for your children if you need to relocate
- List potential people who can help you with your children
- Monitor your family emotional wellbeing

Social
- Get familiar with the new neighbourhood
- List potential people who can help you financially
- Evaluate your support network
- Look for new leisure activities to meet new people
- List potential people who can help you with your daily chores

Work
- Look for a job if not employed
- Apply for a higher position to increase your income
- Consider a carrier change if income is insufficient
- Look for additional part time work to supplement your income

ONE

Why Divorce

"I like the dreams of the future better than the history of the past".
Thomas Jefferson

The Purpose

The purpose of this chapter is to explain the different causes of divorce as well its most common emotional reactions and their impact on your life.

Introduction

Divorce is one of the most significant and traumatic events for any married person. Divorce usually has a direct impact on the nuclear family as well as on the extended family, and directly affects the physical, emotional, social and financial wellbeing of each divorcing individual.

Today, divorce is a common phenomenon which affects families from all walks of life. In the US, more than 90 percent of Americans will get married at least once in their lifetimes. However, staggering statistical data revealed by Olson indicates that almost 50% of the people who get married in the US will end up divorced.

According to the Census Bureau Report on marital status released in 1995, the number of divorced people in the US quadrupled from 4.3 million in 1970 to 18.3 million in 1995.

In the US alone, 1.2 million couples get divorced each year. This figure has a serious financial and economic impact. It was calculated by B. Scafidi that the overall annual cost of divorces to the US economy is estimated to be around $112 billion.

In addition to the global financial impact of divorce on the national economy, it also has a direct financial impact on the divorcing couple and their families. According to Olson, divorced couples tend to be much poorer than their married counterparts, with a median household net worth of approximately $ 33.000 compared to $132.000 for married couples.

According to P. Terrance, children from single-parent homes have a higher probability of growing up in poverty and having a reduced quality of life, and show higher rates of substance abuse and crime involvement compared to children who grow up in traditional households.

In addition, according to R. Colman, children who grow up in traditional two-parent homes tend to be emotionally healthier and to attain higher academic achievements than children from divorced homes.

According to Deutsche, the higher divorce figure is not exclusively confined to the US. Generally, divorce rates are on the rise internationally. In Germany, for example, the divorce rates have risen beyond 200,000 a year, affecting over 400,000 spouses and 170,000 school-aged children.

A similar trend of increased divorce rates was also reported in the UK by the Office of National Statistics. According to the data published in 2004, the total number of divorces in England and Wales was 13.9 divorces per 1000 married people. This number represents a substantial increase from the 2002 figure which was 13.4 divorces per 1000 married people.

Statistics Canada reported that during 2003 the total number of men getting divorces was 16.2 %. This figure represents a significant increase from the 5.2% divorce rate reported in 1973. The Canadian national divorce rate rose by 1% in 2003, reaching an annual amount of 70,828 divorce cases. These statistical figures clearly demonstrate an overall and significant increase in the divorce rates internationally, affecting millions of people worldwide.

Figure 1.1 depicts data reported by the Americans for divorce reform which shows the percentage of divorces in new marriages during 2002 internationally. It appears that the divorce rates figures seem to be much lower in developing countries which have a stronger religious orientation, compared to developed nations which have less religious orientation.

Fig.1.1   International Divorce Rates as % of New Marriages

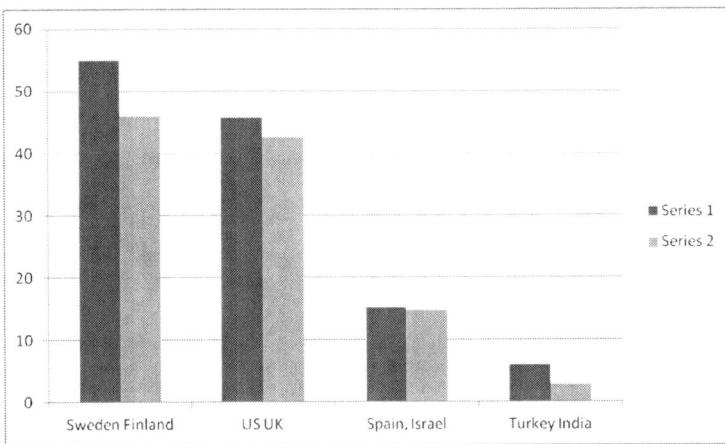

Effect of Age and the Length of Marriage on Divorce

Contrary to the commonly held belief that younger couples are more prone to divorce, the average age at which couples separate is steadily increasing. The current figures which were reported in 2004, by the UK office of National Statistics showed that the average age of divorce is 42

15

years for men, and 39 years for women.

The likelihood of getting a divorce reduces for men and woman after the age of 60 years. US data published by the Bureau of the Census in 1995, showed that the probability to divorce at a higher age is only 36% compared to the figure of 50% of divorce rates in younger couples. In the US, the National Center for Health Statistics reported that 43% of first marriages end in separation or divorce within the first 15 years of marriage. Furthermore, the US Census Bureau predicts that 50% of marriages taking place right now will eventually end up in divorce. The commonly held belief that marriages are more susceptible to ending in divorce during the early years of marital life is also incorrect. Data published in 1995 by the Census Bureau show that within the first 5 years, only 10% of marriages are expected to end in divorce. However, the divorce figures increase to 20% after 10 years of marriage.

These statistical data indicate that divorce has been increasing globally over the past 10 years, and that it can affect any age group, involving millions of lives and causing severe financial hardships to the families involved, as well as constituting a major economic burden to society as a whole.

The reasons for divorce are numerous and will be discussed in the following section.

THEN WHY DO PEOPLE GET DIVORCED?

Marital Dissatisfaction

Each divorce case is unique and has reasons specific to the parting couple. However, often the actual reasons leading to the dissolution of the marriage are unknown, and more commonly are totally different from the reasons stated in the official legal documents.

The discrepancy between the official version and the actual reasons for divorce is often the result of the pressured need to complete a fast and successful divorce application.

In most divorce cases, marital dissatisfaction was found to be the most common cause of divorce. It is obvious that not all marriages fail for the same reasons, nor is there one reason for all divorces. A study conducted by Mark Pattison in 2001 at the Creighton University Center for Marriage and Family suggests that *time, sex and money* are the biggest obstacles to marital satisfaction among newlywed couples. This study also found that couples with financial problems due to debt incurred prior to the marriage, were at a higher risk of divorce.

In addition, marital dissatisfaction was strongly affected by the couple's inability to balance work with family life. This factor had a major influence on the marriage quality which often resulted in multiple conflicts. On the other hand, younger couples under the age of 29 years reported having higher marital dissatisfaction, mainly due to disagreement regarding the frequency of sex.

The main obstacles to marital satisfaction in couples above the age of 30 years were the constant bickering and the different expectations about household tasks. Often, those marital dissatisfaction factors emanated from poor marital communication styles.

Although, money, sex and time are cited as the most common reasons for marital arguments, the principal factor that leads to marital dissatisfaction is not *what* the couple argues about, but *how* they argue. General conflict mismanagement is the biggest cause of marital dissatisfaction, which often bears the seeds for future divorce.

Causes of Marital Dissatisfaction

As I mentioned earlier, divorce has multiple causes. Dissatisfaction with the marriage usually causes multiple conflicts which do not necessarily lead to divorce. The causes that can potentially lead to divorce are usually major events or conflicts over important issues.

The following list includes the most common factors that lead to divorce:

- Poor communication
- Financial difficulties
- Infidelity
- Substance abuse
- Physical, emotional abuse
- Poor conflict resolution skills
- Failed expectations from the marriage
- Lack of commitment
- Conflicts over frequency of sex
- Uncompromising attitude over important issues
- Irreconcilable values
- Incompatible differences

Poor Marital Communication Style

Couples with poor basic communication skills tend to exacerbate a minor issue transforming it into a major fight. Poor communication leads to misunderstandings that result in emotional break-ups. Major communication meltdown results from the couple's inability to express their views and opinions clearly.

The lack of communication skills emanates from the inability to limit the argument to a specific issue only. Such couples tend to bring into the conflict other additional issues that belong to unrelated conflicting areas of the marriage.

In addition, a couple with poor communication skills tends to express their views negatively, without bringing alternative suggestions or different solutions to the problem at hand. Such couples tend to accuse one another for failure to attend a required event or to complete a needed task, and often fail to listen and accept explanations or excuses.

In the case of a partner failing to complete a required task, the accuser tends to blame his/her partner for failing to attend to a required task, and immediately brings up additional criticism regarding his/her inability to complete other tasks, and to add spice to the argument, s/he also blames the lack or dysfunction on his/her partner's "defective" personality.

The following vignette is an example of a dysfunctional marital communication:

Jack arrived back home without the milk and bread that his wife Jane had asked him to buy. The following exchange of words followed immediately: "Where is the milk? Don't tell me you forgot to buy milk? I can't believe it, you ALWAYS forget to do what I ask, you are too lazy and self-centred". Jack responds angrily and sarcastically, "The shop was closed, but anyway it doesn't matter, you always shout and blame me no matter what I do". This exchange or verbal assault is typical of a couple with poor communication skills, as each blames the other and jumps to conclusions instead of asking for the facts.

Another dysfunctional communication style involves an extensive use of mind-reading. Mind-reading is a common phenomenon in which each spouse knows what his/her spouse is thinking without the needed verbal input to validate it. Pursuant to such a communication style, there is no attempt to find out or to validate the assumption made. Excessive use of mind-reading results in misunderstanding, and often leads to the wrong conclusion.

Dysfunctional marital communication generates tension and promotes emotional distance. Usually, the negative impact of poor communication gets worse during stressful times and also deteriorates during conflicts.

In addition, it is extremely hard to create an emotional bond without having functional and positive verbal communication. Dissatisfied couples rarely make regular eye contact, and tend to be physically distant from one another. In a couple that resorts to a negative, non-verbal communication style, physical gestures are used to express negative emotions, anger and coldness.

Financial Difficulties

Financial difficulties create a tremendous pressure on any relationship. The lack of money needed for daily expenses is a huge source of pressure that often translates into marital conflicts. Past debts brought into the marriage generate additional pressure on the marriage.

Infidelity and Lack of Commitment

Spousal infidelity is seldom accepted as a normal event. More frequently, infidelity becomes a huge issue which often results in divorce. However, in many abusive relationships, infidelity is often accepted by the spouse who is cheated upon, as it is an example of abuse. In such an abusive relationship, the abusive, domineering spouse disregards his/her partner's feelings and forms relationships outside the marriage which represent a form of emotional abuse in order to gratify his/her own personal needs.

On the other hand, there are marriages of convenience in which both parties are already emotionally separated. In such a relationship, an extramarital affair is not viewed as a form of infidelity.

In general, infidelity is regarded as less offensive if it occurs as a once-off limited event. On the other hand, a long term love affair (relationship) is likely to be less acceptable to a betrayed spouse.

Substance Abuse, Physical and Emotional Abuse

A substance-abusing partner always causes severe marital, financial, emotional and legal problems. A spouse who excessively abuses drugs or alcohol is often dysfunctional, and tends to exploit the family's financial resources, potentially endangering his/her family, either by getting involved with criminal elements who supply the drugs, or by resorting to criminal activities. Sometimes, heavy abuse of drugs and or alcohol is coupled with physical and emotional abuse. In such circumstances, there is an urgent need for immediate intervention, and in many cases divorce will be the best solution.

Irreconcilable Differences and Incompatible Values

Some marriages are characterised by the presence of severe personality incompatibility. Such couples have opposite value systems which regularly results in conflict. Although there are many married couples who hold different views about different life issues and are still able to have a stable marriage, more commonly, having a completely opposite value system will lead to conflicts and to divorce.

Saving Battered Relationships

A survey conducted by V. Dicarion and reported by the National Fatherhood

Initiative at the University of Texas in Austin regarding the effort made by divorcing couples to save their marriages, revealed that, contrary to the conventional expectations that divorce occurs only after the couple have tried their utmost to save their marriage, in the majority of cases, divorce occurred without any serious attempt made by the couple to work on the marriage problem areas.

Key Points

- Divorce is a common and increasing international phenomenon.
- A divorce can lead to serious emotional reactions.
- A divorce has many causes which include poor communication, infidelity, financial problems, and having irreconcilable values.
- The presence of emotional or physical abuse is a major cause of divorce.
- Divorcing couples rarely attempt to save their marriages before they start the divorce process.

References

1. Olson, D., Olson, A., Larson, P. (2008). *The couple checkup.* Thomas Nelson.
2. Scafidi, B. (2008). *The taxpayer cost of divorce and unwed childbearing.* New York: Institute for American Values.
3. Terrance, P. (1999). *Family disruption and delinquency.* Bulletin, Office of Juvenile Justice and Delinquency Prevention, US Department of Justice, September.

4. Colman, R., Widom, C.S. (2004) Childhood abuse and neglect and adult intimate relationships: A prospective study. *Child Abuse and Neglect*, 28, No. 11:1133 – 1151.

5. Deutsche Welle. 09.29.2005. *Divorce at Germany Newstands.*

6. UK Office of National Statistics. 2004. Cited in a posting from Smart Marriages Listserv August 31.2004.

7. United Press International, March 9, 2005.

8. Bramlet, Matthew and Mosher, W. ( ). First marriage dissolution, divorce and remarriage: US advanced data. *Vital and Health Statistics, No. 323.* Hyattsville MD: National Center for Health Statistics: 21.

9. Washington DC: Bureau of the Census, September 1995, XiX, Table K.

10. Pattison, M. (2001). [online] Available at www.Creighton.edu/ MarriageandFamily/. [Accessed in a citation from a posting from Smart marriages Listserv].

11. Dicarion,V. (2005). NFI releases report on National Marriage Survey. *Fatherhood Today,* Vol 10, Issue 3: 4-5. [Online] [Available at www.fatherhood.org].

12. Prochaska, J. O., Diclemente, C.C. (1982). Transtheorethical therapy: Toward a more integrative model of change. *Psychotherapy: Theory, Research and Practice,* 19: 276-288.

13. Crowe, M. (2005). *Overcoming relationship problems: A self-help guide using CBT.* London: Robinson.

14. Scarf, M. (1987). *Intimate Partners.* New York: Random House.

15. Wegscheider-Cruse, S. (1994). *Life After Divorce.* Health Communication, Inc.

16. Oberlin, L.H. (2005). *Surviving Separation and Divorce.* Adams Media, an F+ W Publication.

TWO

The Divorce Process

"We are in the bondage to the law in order that we may be free."
Cicero

The Purpose

The purpose of this chapter is to explain the divorce emotional process.

The Effects of Divorce Pathways

The divorce proceeds along three separate pathways.

- The emotional path
- The psychological path
- The legal path

In practical terms, a divorce is a legal procedure that leads to the marriage dissolution which is technically similar to a partnership dissolution. However, due to the emotional and psychological complexities, the divorce is far more complicated than that of a simple business transaction.

In most cases, the divorce is not a sudden event. Usually, the divorce starts long before the legal part commences due to psychological and emotional problems. The need for divorce is often the result of a psychological and emotional desire for a change in one or in both spouses.

The Emotional Path

The divorce process generates many emotional reactions which commonly develop in both divorcing spouses. The most common emotional reactions to divorce are shock reactions, anxiety, depression and anger. A successful resolution of the divorce emotional reaction results in acceptance. Emotional acceptance is the final emotional stage, and represents the desired goal of a healthy divorce in which both parties are able to emotionally accept the finality of their relationship, and are capable of moving forward in life emotionally.

As mentioned earlier, the decision to get a divorce is rarely a sudden event. In most divorce cases, the couple has severe unmet emotional needs that initiate the emotional process. The divorce-related emotional reactions include at least three distinctive stages, which, once they have materialised, can lead to an emotional decision to get a divorce.

The divorce emotional stages are:

- The stage of emotional erosion
- The selfishness stage
- The stage of emotional break-up

Each emotional stages proceeds, eventually, to the development of a strong emotional desire to make an emotional change. The emotional decision for a change provides the energy required to initiate the divorce process.

Stage One
The Stage of Emotional Erosion

The emotional erosion is the first stage in the emotional process that leads to divorce. It starts with emotional dissatisfaction with the marriage which develops in one or in both spouses. The emotional erosion starts with a growing disappointment in the marriage, the spouse's behaviour and attitude. Doubt over the viability of the marital relationship takes over the initial enthusiasm and the automatic acceptance of the spouse's behaviour.

The thought, "This marriage is not what I expected and wished for" becomes more frequent, and joins other eroding questions such as, "Why do I need this?" and "Why can't I do what I really want to do?", or "I deserve a better partner than this couch potato".

Common to this initial stage is the development of the feeling that the person you married is different from the one you bargained on. Normally, at this stage, the marriage transforms into an unpleasant battlefield. Feelings of resentment and disappointment usually fuel the frequent marital conflicts. Blaming each other is a method used to justify one's behaviour and the interpersonal impasse. Past feelings of love and happiness change after endless fights into feelings of unhappiness, resentment, and bitterness, and often culminate in feelings of hate.

Stage Two
The Emotional Selfishness Stage

Emotional selfishness is the second stage in the emotional process that leads to divorce. It usually begins with emotional distance, as both spouses feel emotionally distant from one another. This emotional gap is quickly filled with an emotional 'wall' that further distances each spouse from the other.

The positive emotional energy that used to cement the relationship transforms into a negative emotion which includes feelings of hate, disappointment and resentment. The love experienced during the early marital life largely dissipates and turns into mutual disappointment.

The initial positive emotional energy which was invested in the relationship with the spouse becomes redirected towards the self. Each spouse starts to prioritise his/her own personal interests over those of his/her spouse. Each spouse feels more comfortable being alone or with friends, than with his/her spouse. Decisions regarding day- to-day activities are taken unilaterally without considering or consulting the spouse. An example of emotional selfishness is whenever you think, "I deserve to have a holiday, and if s/he refuses to join me then tough luck". Another example of emotional selfishness is when you start to go out alone or with friends or other family members.

Stage Three
The Emotional Break-up Stage

The emotional break-up stage is the final emotional stage in the divorce path. This stage often begins with the presence of emotional indifference to your spouse's needs and wellbeing. The impact of your behaviour on your spouse is considered irrelevant, and hurting your spouse doesn't worry you anymore. Having emotional indifference to your spouse's emotional life and needs often manifests in a total lack of involvement or interest in his/her life. The communication breakdown often follows the emotional breakdown, and results in a complete and total disinterest in your spouse. His/her life becomes his/her problem and not a joint marital problem.

Such an emotional disengagement process can develop either mutually in both spouses, or unilaterally, in one spouse only. In either event, the emotional disengagement process culminates in emotional divorce, which is a necessary and indispensable step in the divorce process.

However, the emotional disengagement process that fuels the decision to get a divorce often generates additional emotional reactions, which may include feelings of anxiety, depression, guilt, low self-esteem and anger. Most of those emotional reactions to the divorce process are dysfunctional in the sense that they can affect negatively your level of functioning, and your ability to cope with your daily needs. It is important to be able to identify those dysfunctional emotional responses, and to manage them as quickly, and as adequately as possible, since a healthy emotional life is crucial to reaching a successful divorce outcome. An adequate control of your dysfunctional emotions will have a positive influence on your children and extended family members' emotional life.

The Psychological Path

The psychological path proceeds parallel to the emotional path. The psychological process starts with the spouse who develops a strong psychological need for change. The need for a psychological change progresses along several steps which will be described later in the chapter and will eventually end with an action taken towards separation.

The Psychological Process of Change

As I explained earlier, the reasons for divorce are multiple, and differ from couple to couple. However, the final decision to get a divorce has a common psychological denominator which is the presence of a strong psychological need for a change.

The need to make a life change requires a complicated psychological process which has several separate and distinctive stages. The various

psychological stages leading to change were extensively researched by
Prochaska & DiClemente. Although Prochaska's theoretical model was
developed primarily for those who have a problem with addiction, it can be
adapted to the divorce situation. According to Prochaska's psychological
model of change, the final decision to take an action is preceded by
several psychological phases. Each psychological phase requires the
accomplishment of a specific task before one can move on to the next
phase. The entire model is illustrated in Figure 2.2.

Fig 2.2   **The Model of Psychological Change Adapted from
Prochaska**

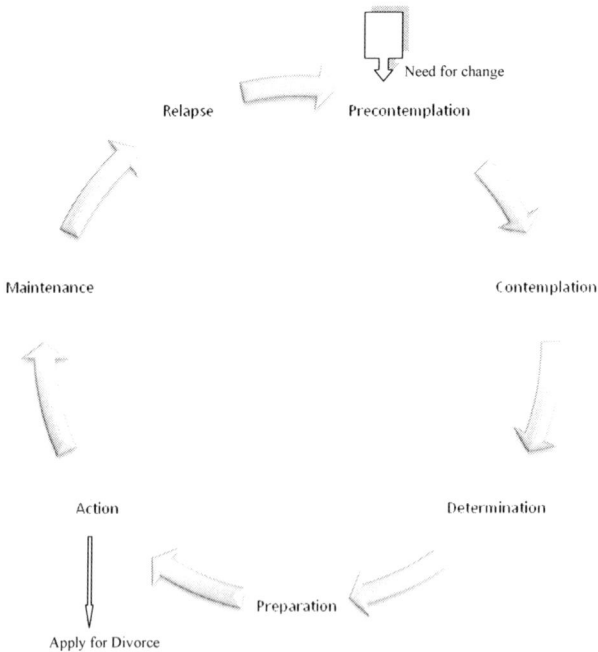

Permanent exit represents the ability to go through the divorce process
and to start a new life. (Adapted from Prochaska)

A detailed analysis of the different psychological phases of change shows that each phase requires a successful resolution of the previous phase. Once all phases are successfully accomplished, then a psychological change becomes permanent, and can lead to an action which is, in your case, a divorce.

A successful resolution of the different psychological phases creates the right atmosphere for a change and is vital for initiating the divorce.

A) *The pre-contemplation phase*

The pre-contemplation phase is the initial phase which can lead to a change and which propels you to take an action. During the marriage, there are strong psychological forces of denial working in full swing to prevent any change, and to maintain the *status quo*. You often deny the existence of marital problems, and you are unaware of the dysfunctional relationship that exists in your marriage.

B) *The contemplation phase*

The contemplation phase has two parts. The first part starts with the realisation that there are some problems in your marriage. You might initially have thoughts such as, "Something is not okay if we disagree and fight all the time", or "We are both unhappy and miserable". Acknowledging that something must be done to change the situation is part of this contemplation phase. During this phase, the need to make a change in the current marriage is finally acknowledged. In the second part of the contemplation phase, you start making a preliminary investigations regarding divorce procedures and other divorce requirements, as well as considering the possible consequences of your divorce.

C) *The determination phase*

The determination phase is the psychological phase in which the decision to take action is finally reached. You firmly believe that change in the marriage is the only answer to your dysfunctional marriage.

D) *The preparation phase*

The preparation phase is the phase in which you start thinking about the different options and actions needed to be taken in order to change your life. In other words, you start thinking about what you must do in order to get divorced.

E) *The action phase*

This is the action time. You finally take the first step which will result in divorce. The various actions you take include visiting a divorce lawyer, opening a separate bank account, meeting with a financial consultant, looking for new accommodation and for a new school for your children.

F) *The maintenance phase*

The maintenance phase is the phase in which your new life as a separated, divorced individual starts. This phase involves the acquisition of new friends, independent employment and management of your daily requirements without your ex-spouse's intervention. Your life as an independent individual starts at this point.

Ideally, during the psychological process of change, the movement through the different phases is unidirectional until you can reach the desired action phase. However, relapse is common, and inevitable. You can easily fall back from any achieved phase into a previously lower phase.

For example, during the contemplation phase one may often already be convinced that one needs to change one's life and must get a divorce. However, one's mind may often be changed due to severe financial difficulties or due to family pressure, and one can then fall back to the pre-contemplation phase and wonder whether divorce is really a good option.

Setbacks are inevitable and expected, but you must not be discouraged by them. You constantly need to re-evaluate your position and strive to move up the psychological change ladder, if deemed appropriate, until you reach your final goal which is a better life for you and your family.

Adapting Prochaska's model to the divorce scenario allows you to identify your own position. In other words, you can identify where you stand psychologically, regarding your marriage.

Table 2.3 has several examples, which provide you with a better conceptual framework regarding the need for change.

Table 2.3   Example of the Psychological Phases Adapted to the Divorce Process

The phases of change	Examples of what can happen to you in each phase
Pre-contemplation phase	This is when you are in denial and are still unable to comprehend the magnitude of your marital problems. At this stage you might say to yourself, *"My marriage is okay. I don't have a problem"*.
Contemplation phase	*This occurs when you realise that something may be wrong with your marriage. At this stage you might ask yourself, "What should I do to change my life?"*

Determination phase	*This happens when you are pretty sure that your marital problems are unsolvable. At this stage you have already made up your mind to end your marriage.*
Preparation phase	*This takes place when you make the decision to take action. At this stage you may say to yourself, "I need to do ... tonight", or when you meet with the real estate agent to look for a house, or when you open a new private bank account.*
Action phase	*This occurs when you actually leave the family home.*
Maintenance phase	*This happens when you start getting used to a single life. For example, you start going out for coffee with a friend.*
Relapse phase	*This occurs when you regret the change you made and you look for ways to go back to your spouse. For example, you convince yourself that you can move back to your spouse because he promised to change".*

Thinking about divorce action plan

By now you may have gained some insight into the causes that can lead to divorce, and to the psychological and emotional phases that you are required to reach before you can take adequate steps. The following action plan flow chart will help you identify your current psychological position.

Figure 2.4   The Action Plan Flow Chart:

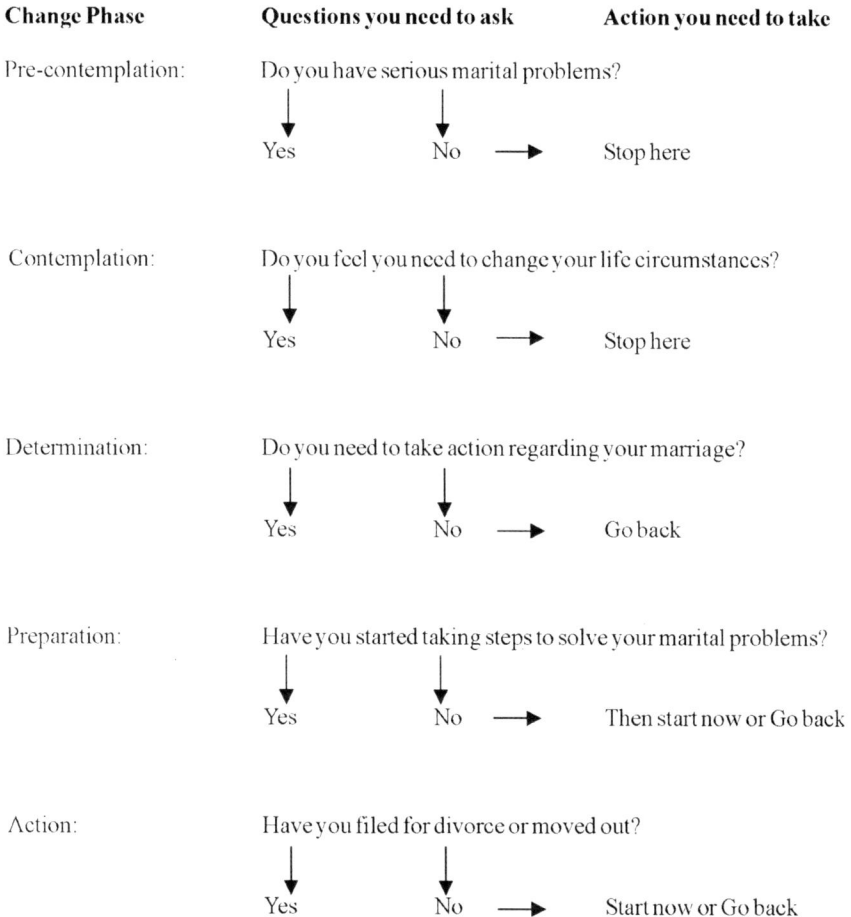

Change Phase	Questions you need to ask	Action you need to take

Pre-contemplation: Do you have serious marital problems?

Yes   No → Stop here

Contemplation: Do you feel you need to change your life circumstances?

Yes   No → Stop here

Determination: Do you need to take action regarding your marriage?

Yes   No → Go back

Preparation: Have you started taking steps to solve your marital problems?

Yes   No → Then start now or Go back

Action: Have you filed for divorce or moved out?

Yes   No → Start now or Go back

Upon completion of the flow chart, you may find out whether you are heading forward towards making a life change, or falling backwards toward the *status quo* state. Remember that a change in your marital status will affect your family at every conceivable level. Therefore, before you make changes in your marital status, you need to carefully evaluate the possible effects of such a move.

The Legal Path

The legal path often initiates long after the emotional and the psychological path starts. The legal process involves a working relationship with a legal team which will file, on behalf of the divorcing couple, the court application. The legal process that ensues leads to the marriage termination. The divorce paper signed by the judge upon completion of a comprehensive and acceptable settlement will be accepted by the divorcing couple, and will seal the divorce as final. The interaction between the three divorce pathways is illustrated in Figure 2.5.

Figure 2.5   The Divorce Pathways

Again, please take note that change is not always good. The following chapter will help you shed some light on the consequences of the divorce for you and your family. In addition, it will help you to gain a clearer insight into the practicality of divorce.

Key Points

*   The divorce proceeds along emotional, psychological and legal pathways
*   Adaptation of Prochaska's psychological model of change can help you to identify your readiness to divorce.

References

1. Prochaska, J.O., Diclemente, C.C. (1982). Transtheorethical therapy: Toward a more integrative model of change. *Psychotherapy: Theory, Research and Practice*, 19: 276-288.
2. Crowe, M. (2005). Overcoming relationship problems: A self-help guide using CBT. London: Robinson.
3. Scarf, M. (1987). *Intimate Partners*. New York: Random House.
4. Wegscheider-Cruse, S. (1994). *Life After Divorce*. Health Communication, Inc.
5. Oberlin, L.H. (2005). *Surviving Separation and Divorce*. Adams Media, an F+ W Publication.

THREE

Considering Divorce

"Let him that would move the world, first move himself".
Socrates

The Purpose

The purpose of this chapter is to explain the factors you need to consider before you apply for divorce.

The divorce is a complicated process which might have a multiple emotional and practical impact on you and your family. Before you start thinking about divorce, you need to gain some insight into the practical effects of the divorce on you and your family. Completing the following questionnaire might provide a better insight into such a difficult decision.

Evaluating the Divorce Consequences

1. Do you have children: Yes / No _____

2. Which child will live with you after the divorce and why?
    Name: _____

Name: _____

Name: _____

Name: _____

Name: _____

3. If your children will stay with your spouse will you be able to see
    them regularly? Yes / NO _____

4. How frequently will you be able to see your children? _____
    _____
    _____

5. Your profession: _____

6. Your current work situation: _____
    Unemployed: Yes / No _____
    Part time job: Yes / No _____
    Full time job: Yes / No _____
    Realistic expectation of getting a job: Yes / No _____
    Required hours: _____

7. Your current financial income: _____

8. Your future predicted income: _____

9. Your future predicted monthly expenses: Total: _____
    On Housing: _____
    On Children's Maintenance: _____
    On Food: _____
    On Children's Education: _____
    On Transport: _____
    On Recreation: _____
    On Municipality Taxes: _____
    On Clothing: _____

10. Living conditions: _____

Can you stay in the same family home?   Yes / No _____
Do you need to look for a new house?   Yes / No _____

11.   Social life: You predict that you will have the following social network after divorce: _____
Name: _____
Name: _____
Name: _____
Name: _____
Name: _____

12.   You predict losing the following friends:
Name: _____
Name: _____
Name: _____
Name: _____

Getting a divorce also requires additional changes such as:
•   The need to organise transfer of your possessions
•   The need to look for a nearby school for your children (if relevant)
•   The need to find new directions to your workplace
•   The need to look for the availability of local amenities such as department stores, local health care professionals, post offices and local banks

Once you have managed to establish your readiness for marital change and its implications, you also need to consider what losses and what gains you should expect from the divorce.

What are the Expected Divorce Losses?

While you examine the different consequences of your divorce you need to ask yourself what aspect of your life will be negatively affected by the divorce. In particular, you need to consider what the possible divorce losses will be. The losses in divorce can be multiple, extending to multiple areas of your life. In general, your divorce losses can be separated into three principal domains:

- Personal losses
- Interpersonal losses
- Financial losses

The various divorce-related losses are summarised in Figure 3.1.

Fig 3.1   The Divorce-Related Losses

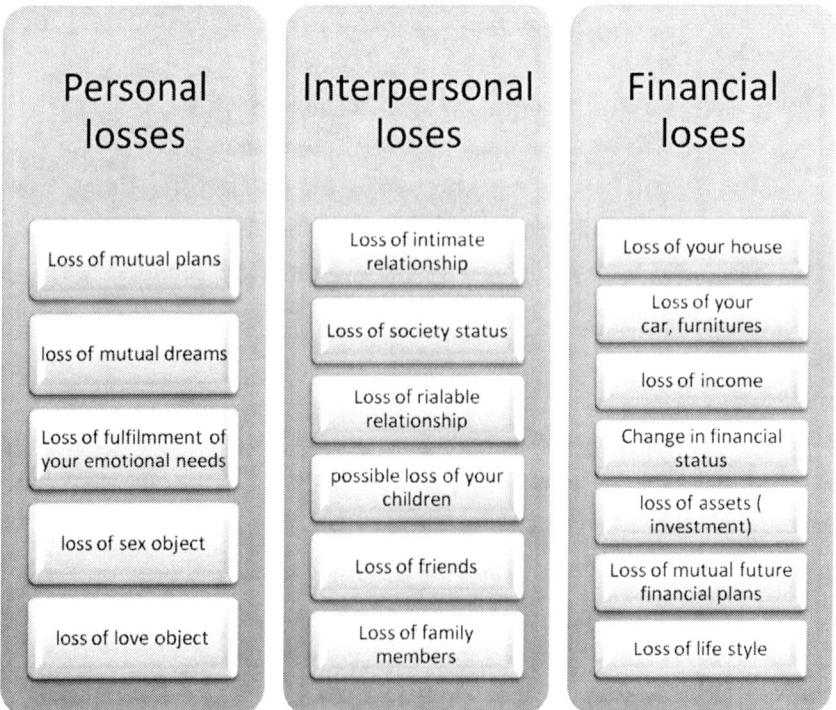

Personal losses	Interpersonal loses	Financial loses
Loss of mutual plans	Loss of intimate relationship	Loss of your house
loss of mutual dreams	Loss of society status	Loss of your car, furnitures
Loss of fulfilment of your emotional needs	Loss of rialable relationship	loss of income
loss of sex object	possible loss of your children	Change in financial status
loss of love object	Loss of friends	loss of assets (investment)
	Loss of family members	Loss of mutual future financial plans
		Loss of life style

Divorce-related losses can heavily influence your emotional state and your overall view about getting a divorce. Some of the losses will take place immediately you start the divorce process, while other losses might be more on the virtual sphere and have a limited impact on you and your family.

Examples of a virtual loss are the effect of divorce on your social status. Often a virtual perceived loss can be as crippling as a real loss. The following exercise will, again require your active participation in order to evaluate your potential divorce losses as well as their significance to you.

Table 3.2   What are Your Potential Divorce Losses?

Aspects that will be affected by the divorce	Personal Importance Not important Very important 0---------5----------10	Your level of confidence to overcome the loss Not confident Very confident 0----------5----------10
Financial Loss		
Example: "I might need to sell my house".	8	10
Example: "I might lose my car".	10	5

Personal loss		
Example: "Finally I can be free from my alcoholic aggressive spouse".	10	2
Interpersonal loss		
Example: "I might lose my friends".	6	3
Example: "I might lose contact with my in-laws".	5	2

What are the Potential Divorce Gains?

Getting a divorce also has its own advantages. Divorce can represent a new beginning, and a departure from past crippling relationships into a potentially new, functional life. New working possibilities can be considered along with new relationships, a new lifestyle and a new financial status. The following Table, 3.3 will help you to evaluate the potential gains you can achieve by getting a divorce.

Table 3.3   My Potential Divorce Gains Log

Life aspects that will be affected by the change	Personal Importance Not important Very important 0-----------5-----------10	Your level of confidence in coping with the divorce gain Not confident Very confident 0-----------5----------10
Financial gain		
Example: "I will have my own house".	10	7
Example: "I will finally get my own car".	8	5

Personal gains		
Example: "Finally I can start a relationship based on mutual respect and security".	10	2
Example: "I will strengthen my relationship with my family".	5	2
Inter-personal gains		
Example: "I will acquire new friends".	9	7

Example: "I will finally get to live closer to my family".	8	10

So, after evaluating your readiness for change and the potential divorce losses and gains you can refine your dilemma, and decide whether you are ready for the big change and whether to get a divorce or not? For this final evaluation, you also need to look at the overall pros and the cons of getting a divorce. The following exercise requires you to gather your thoughts regarding the pros and cons of maintaining the current *status quo* or opting to change your marital status.

For this purpose, you are required to complete Table 3.4. Each issue you need to consider is based on its importance to *you*, which is totally different for every individual, so asking advice from friends or family might be misleading. In addition, you might change your perspective daily, dependent on your mood and your life circumstances. Pursuant to such possible daily variations, you should re-evaluate your position at different time frames. Displaying similar scores for each item in different time frames can validate your views regarding the divorce, while changing your score frequently might call into question your readiness for divorce.

Dr Shlomo Brook

Table 3.4: **The Pros and Cons of Maintaining the *Status Quo* or Making a Change.**

Pros *status quo* option	Personal Value Score 0 ------- 5 ------ 10 Min. Max.	Date	Date	Date
1.				
2.				
3.				
4.				
5.				
Cons *status quo* option				
1.				
2.				
3.				
4.				
5.				

Another important point to consider regarding the divorce relates to the dilemma of whether you should be the first to apply for divorce, or whether you should wait until your spouse makes the first move. The decision to either be the Leaver or the passive one who is dragged into the divorce, is difficult, and merits some careful consideration.

The Leaver Dilemma

The divorce initiator, the Leaver, needs to consider additional factors that might affect his/her life. Each individual in the marriage, as in any other human relationship, stands on a different emotional shelf. Often, both spouses stand on a similar emotional stage and have a similar attitude towards the relationship and the marriage. It is quite natural that one spouse is less satisfied with the marriage compared to the other. Usually, the most dissatisfied spouse becomes the Leaver.

Being the first to apply for divorce carries some advantages as well as several disadvantages which requires additional careful assessment.

The Disadvantage of Being the Leaver

- Fear of being misunderstood
- Fear of being judged as selfish
- Fear of losing mutual friends
- Fear of financial loss
- Fear of losing your children
- Fear of hurting your children
- Dealing with the feelings of guilt and shame that are exclusive to the leaver

The Advantages of Being the Leaver

- Stop spending futile emotional energy on a broken dysfunctional relationship
- Gain a legal headstart: be the first to make legal arrangements
- Get a financial headstart: be the first to make financial arrangements
- Be the first to make new living arrangements
- Have a psychological advantage: a faster adaptation to a new life as a single
- Gain control of the situation by not being controlled by unfolding events

Completing Table 3.5 will help you to gain better insight into the advantages or disadvantages of becoming the Leaver. Yet again, your point of view might change frequently. Therefore, you need to re-evaluate the advantages and the disadvantages at different points of time.

Table 3.5   The Advantages & Disadvantages of Being the Leaver

Advantages of becoming a Leaver	Personal value Score 0 ------ 5 ----- 10 Min. Max.	Date	Date	Date
1.				

2.				
3.				
4.				
5.				
Disadvantages of becoming a Leaver				
1.				
2.				
3.				
4.				
5.				

Optimally, the divorce's different aspects should be carefully weighed up by both spouses before initiating the divorce process. However, more commonly, the most dissatisfied spouse is usually the one who initiates the divorce, while the less dissatisfied spouse is usually the passive spouse who rather follows the unfolding events of the disengagement period.

A divorce decision which is taken mutually commonly occurs in a marriage which has good relationships, a good communication style, and openness. In such marriages, there is a good understanding of each other's needs and the divorce is usually the result of a catastrophic event.

However, in most cases, a unilateral decision to get a divorce is far more common, and usually leads to severe legal, interpersonal and financial conflict.

I hope that this chapter opened your eyes and has helped you gain a better insight into the potential divorce consequences, and the issues you need to consider before you make such an important decision which will affect you and your family.

Key Points

- The divorce can lead to serious losses.
- The divorce can lead to some gains.
- The decision to get a divorce must be carefully considered, and outside advice should have only a limited impact on your decision.
- The Leaver needs to consider additional factors before initiating the divorce.

References

1. Crowe, M. (2005). Overcoming relationship problems: A self-help guide using CBT. London: Robinson.
2. Scarf, M. (1987). *Intimate Partners.* New York: Random House.
3. Wegscheider-Cruse, S. (1994). *Life After Divorce.* Health Communication, Inc.
4. Oberlin, L.H. (2005). *Surviving Separation and Divorce.* Adams Media, an F+ W Publication.

FOUR

Your Divorce Triggers

"A true friend is one who overlooks your failures and
tolerates your successes".
Doug Larson

The Purpose

The purpose of this chapter is to evaluate the divorce triggers with a special focus on your personal circumstances.

Introduction

Divorce is an extremely unpleasant life event which marks the end of an interpersonal relationship as well as the end of your family unit. Divorce will have a dramatic effect on every single member of your family and will substantially change your daily activities and your future plans.

The impact of divorce can range from a minor effect which is hardly noticed, to a colossal effect which leads to a monumental impact on each family member's life and on their future plans. In general, except for being involved with abusive relationships, divorce more often has a negative impact on family members.

The divorce requires you to make a massive change and a major adaptation. Your financial status is usually the first victim of the divorce. You will often have to sell your home due to limited funds, and may have to relocate to a less affluent area and to a smaller home.

Relocating to another area may require you to transfer your children to a new school which means they will have to make new friends. These changes are highly challenging and require massive adaptation. In addition, your previous lifestyle will change drastically. This means that from this day forward, you will drive a smaller car, and you may have to go to a cheaper summer holiday resort and may have less money to spend on unnecessary items.

Besides the financial impact of divorce, there is also a social impact which will affect every member of your family. Your social status will change automatically when you become single. In many societies, being single is often viewed negatively, especially in less developed countries. Being single and divorced might make you feel socially outcast. The single, divorced woman sometimes becomes the sexual target of any male who is looking for an easy score.

Once your social status changes you will quickly discover that many of your male friends will view you as a sex object, whereas married female friends will consider you a potential threat to their own marriages. As a single and divorced woman you will suddenly receive fewer invitations to your friends' houses, and more calls from sexually interested males.

However, divorce is not always negative. In many instances, the divorce can positively change your life. This is specifically true of abusive marriages. Moving away from an abusive relationship is always a positive event which overshadows any other factor. In abusive marriages, the divorce holds the promise of a new beginning which may hopefully lead to a better life and an abuse-free relationship.

The Early Signs of an Unravelling Relationship

The reasons that eroded the marriage and broke up the relationship are multiple and rarely sudden. The divorce is often preceded by behavioural signs that start long before they become clearly evident. In this section I will try to evaluate the early behavioural signs of a problematic marriage.

Most marriages that end in divorce often show some behavioural patterns that can signal marital problems. Can we detect such early signs of an unravelling relationship? Are we able to identify the potential warning signs of marital problems that might end in divorce? What are the most common behavioural manifestations of problem relationships?

The early warning signs of marital problems should be suspected when your spouse develops one of the following behavioural patterns:

A) *The increasingly confrontational spouse:*

An increasingly confrontational spouse is one of the earliest signs of a marital problem. Whenever your spouse who was previously a considerate, sensitive and understanding partner suddenly changes and turns into an unpleasantly confrontational creature, you need to start worrying. Whenever your actions or views seem to irritate him automatically, then it's time for you to start wondering what's going on. If any innocent remarks you make are perceived by him/her as an invitation for a verbal fight, and your spouse seems to look for the slightest excuse to initiate a verbal war, then the warning bells should sound loudly.

B) *The uncompromising spouse:*

When your spouse becomes less compromising and more confrontational, this might be a sign of a marital problem. Whenever the compromising and flexible creature you used to call your life partner changes in front of your eyes into an uncompromising war machine, then it's time to start thinking about the relationship. Past and previous disagreements which used to be resolved peacefully in bed become long-gone memories, as current disagreements end up in a state of war until the last drop of blood has been spilled.

C) The spouse who rather spends more time at work or with friends:

When your spouse prefers to spend more time away from you and his/her children, this might be a classical sign of a marital problem. Your newly achieved independence and his/her need for more personal space are often signs of dark clouds over your relationships. When your spouse adopts a new buzzword: "I need more time for myself" as if the long hours, s/he spends daily gazing at the TV screen while completely ignoring your existence don't count as such, then your marriage is in trouble. Similarly, when your spouse suddenly shows increasing interest in the local pub pretending that lifting the heavy beer glasses is a sort of exercise, then the alarm bells should sound. Emotional and physical distance often manifests in the need to spend more time alone, and this could be an early sign of an unravelling relationship.

D) The secretive spouse:

When your spouse becomes secretive and tries to conceal his/her actions then this is usually a serious warning sign of a marital problem. If your male spouse suddenly transforms into a James Bond clone and your knowledge about his whereabouts is minimal, then there is a good reason for you to start to worry. Whenever your female instincts to know where and how your hunter spends his days remain unsatisfied, or whenever a male spouse's instincts to want to know what his cavewoman is doing are gone, then there could be a severe relationship problem.

E) *The sexually phobic spouse:*

If your spouse avoids having sex with you this is a rather unpleasant sign of a marital problem. A sudden, drastic change in your spouse's sexual behaviour should also be a reason for concern. Whenever your sex-machine spouse transforms into a sexually phobic creature, then the antennae of marital problems should be activated. In addition, if your spouse suddenly avoids even the simplest form of affection, such as a touch or a kiss, and behaves as if these are simply a germ-transmitting exercise, it is time for you to wonder about the relationship.

F) *The critical spouse:*

When your spouse becomes highly critical of and irritable with whatever you do or whatever you say, this is a warning sign of marital problems. In such a scenario, if your spouse, who once used to idealise the ground you walked on and the word you uttered, becomes a copy of the New York Times weekend literary critic and criticises your personality, your behaviour, as well as the way you interact with others, then you should start thinking about the possibility that something is not right in your loveboat. Similarly, when your spouse finds fault with the way you dress or the way you look and also criticises your friends and your family, this could be a dangerous sign of marital dissatisfaction.

G) *A relationship with no fun or pleasure:*

The disappearance of fun or pleasure from the marriage is rather a sad sign of marital discord. In many soured relationships, the good times in which you used to enjoy each other's company disappear and the little time spent together is filled with bitter arguments and constant conflicts over almost every issue. If this occurs, then it is time to worry.

H) *The selfish spouse:*

Selfish behaviour is, in general, highly irritating and destructive to any relationship. Whenever your caring spouse changes into a selfish, inconsiderate creature who only thinks about him/herself then you must know that your marriage is in big trouble. In such a scenario, your spouse suddenly discovers the joy of taking care of his/her own personal needs at the expense of those of his family. If your spouse suddenly decides to follow a lifelong dream and goes away to explore the countryside alone, or buys him/herself an unnecessary, expensive gadget despite the presence of financial difficulties, leaving you frustrated and disappointed, then you should be seriously worried about the marriage.

I) *The body-minded spouse*:

When your spouse suddenly becomes excessively obsessed with his/her body and with his/her clothes then there is a reason to re-evaluate what is going on. There is nothing wrong with losing weight, or upgrading the wardrobe. However, a sudden compulsive obsession with personal appearance while completely neglecting your appearance or that of his/her children provides reasonable grounds for concern.

The Divorce Triggers

There are almost unlimited reasons that can lead to divorce. In most divorce cases, the causes for divorce are deeply rooted in an unresolved marital interpersonal issue. Sometimes, the regular daily frictions are topped up by additional incidents that further affect the marriage and could trigger a divorce.

Long term marital discord also tends to accumulate and grow over the years, creating huge pressure on the marriage and can eventually lead to divorce. In many households, neglecting your spouse's needs and resorting to denial regarding the problematic issues is a common way to handle pressure.

However, unresolved marital differences tend to grow in size and to spill over into many other areas. Couples who avoid confrontation have usually found that the small, unresolved problem suddenly grows into a monstrous obstacle. Small differences have a limited effect on the marriage, while big differences tend to disrupt healthy relationships and can potentially culminate in divorce.

Some stable marriages, on the other hand, may have a major catastrophic event that rocks the marital boat and can lead to divorce. In such a scenario, a seismic marital event generates an unresolved situation which can trigger a divorce.

In general, the divorce triggers can be divided into major and minor categories based on their propensity to cause divorce.

The most common *major* divorce triggers are:
- Extramarital relationships
- Financial loss & bankruptcy
- Occupational problems
- Increased use of alcohol / drug abuse
- Emotional abuse
- Physical abuse
- Spouse separate relocation

The most common *minor* divorce triggers are:
- Sudden personal change
- Shifts in personal life values

Dr Shlomo Brook

Extramarital Relationship

According to Crowe, an extramarital relationship is, by far, the most common trigger for divorce, and sexual infidelity has no competition when it comes to marital destruction. According to Scarf, infidelity is a common marital event occurrence, as 55% of married men and 45% of married women reported having an extramarital affair during their marriage, while up to 70% of married couples have a hidden, unreported extramarital affair during the marriage.

In the modern era of female equality, the male exclusivity in the infidelity department has shockingly receded, as more and more females are rapidly closing the infidelity statistical gap.

It is not hard to imagine the damage caused by having an additional individual in the marriage. The reaction of the cheated spouse to the presence of a third person is commonly a mixture of anger, rejection, humiliation, anguish, damaged self-esteem and a feeling of personal inadequacy.

In addition, the presence of a triangular relationship can also increase severe feelings of distrust. Studies show that women tend to get highly upset when they discover that their spouse is emotionally or sexually involved with another woman, yet are more prone to forgiving their partner's infidelity. The male spouse, on the other hand, has a more traditional reaction to his wife's infidelity and, according to Linda Papadopoulos, in most cases males who have been cheated on find this much harder to accept, and experience greater difficulty in healing their damaged egos. According to Linda Papadopoulos, studies show that extramarital affairs are more likely to be a *symptom* than a *cause* of a problem marriage.

Infidelity rarely flourishes in healthy and stable marriages unless both sides have a mutual consensus around the issue of participating in a swinging lifestyle. The length of an extramarital affair also plays an important role in triggering a divorce. A spouse who was engaged in a short-term extramarital relationship can be forgiven much more quickly by the loving spouse, than the spouse who had a long-term extramarital affair, or a spouse who is still engaged in an ongoing extramarital relationship.

In addition, the spouse who has an ongoing extramarital relationship and is unwilling to give up such involvement has fewer probabilities of keeping his marriage intact.

The presence of a third party in the marriage provides additional strain and is rarely accepted by the spouse who is being cheated on. In many cases of infidelity, the spouse engaged in the extramarital relationship often has a previous history of similar behaviour.

At other times, the extramarital affair can be explained either as an attempt to compensate for a dysfunctional relationship or to serve as an act of revenge, or as an attempt to meet unfulfilled needs.

Financial Hardships

Families facing severe financial difficulties or who are on the verge of economic bankruptcy face a higher risk of getting a divorce than families with a stable economic status.

A family experiencing serious financial problems is usually exposed to a higher level of stress which can destroy the marriage.

In such marriages, the main financial providers feel inadequate and commonly have damaged self-esteem. Feelings of failure are common in such a situation, and there is a higher level of mutual disappointment raised from the inability to attain a desired lifestyle. Such presence of disappointment coupled with low self-esteem and failure can translate, eventually, into arguments, mutual accusations and divorce.

Work Overload

Having one or both spouses with an intense work overload is another common factor that can trigger a divorce. The overworked couple often displace the work-related problems onto each other, transforming the family into an extension of the work battleground.

Emotional and Physical Abuse

Emotional and physical abuse is a regular source of stress that can trigger divorce. Abusive relationships often involve a heavy use of alcohol and or drugs. Marriages which suffer ongoing emotional and physical abuse are usually highly dysfunctional. Unfortunately, many cases of abusive marriages tend to last for a long period of time due to the psychological, emotional and economic dependency that is highly common in such relationships.

The abused spouse becomes paralysed and is unable to take the necessary steps, even in the face of life-threatening circumstances. Commonly abusive marriages continue longer than they should due to the presence of extreme fear. In many cases, the abused spouse is financially dependent and has a limited support network to lean on.

Frequently, the abusive marriages normally terminate after an episode of severe violence which results in a long-term jail sentence for the violent spouse. In such an event, the physical marital distance serves as a catalyst and an opportunity to escape from such a destructive relationship.

The Need for Relocation

The relocation of one spouse to another city due to work needs is a common phenomenon, and can also be a common divorce trigger. Another common reason for relocation is caused by a sudden need to help a sick distant parent. In the event of the relocation of one spouse for an extensive period, the single separate lifestyle imposed on both spouses can serve as the catalyst for an emotional separation which might end up in divorce.

Personality Change or Having a Chronic Disability

Personality changes, or having a spouse with a new onset of physical or mental disability is a common cause of divorce. Such eventualities usually increase the levels of stress, and require a major adaptation from the non-affected spouse.

Minor Divorce Triggers

The minor divorce triggers are, in general, less disruptive, and do not usually lead to divorce. Minor triggers can be either a temporary financial problem, or the presence of an occasional pressure-causing event which temporarily affects the family. Such triggers rarely lead to divorce, although minor triggers can have a cumulative effect on the marriage which might make them a more serious trigger of divorce. In addition, the divorce triggers can either be a sudden, short-term event or a chronic, ongoing problem.

What are your Divorce Triggers?

In every broken relationship there are underlying events that can trigger the divorce. Each divorce is unique and has its own triggers specific to the marriage.

Your divorce can be triggered either by a specific, clear, sudden incident, or by unrecognised, ongoing chronic reasons. In most divorce cases, the divorce is triggered by the combination of a sudden event superimposed on several small ongoing chronic circumstances.

Completing Table 4.1 will help you gain a better insight into your divorce-related triggers. The aim of the following exercise is to establish what the triggers are that lead to your marriage break-up. You need to grade each proposed trigger's severity based on its impact on your marriage.

In addition, some events might be massive and unacceptable to YOU. Unacceptable events require a red flag score which implies an irreversible trigger.

Table 4.1   Assessing your Divorce-Related Triggers

Divorce-related Triggers	The impact of the trigger on your marriage: 0----------------10 Minimal impact Maximal	Red flag X
Sudden major marital circumstances:		
1 *example: extramarital affair*	10	X
2		
3		
4		
5		

Chronic ongoing marital circumstances:		
1 *example: your spouse never helps you with the household chores*	7	
2		
3		
4		
5		
Total number of red flags:		

The higher the score you give to the various divorce triggers, the higher the possibility that your marriage is coming to an end. In addition, having a red flag further increases the divorce potential. Emotional and physical abuse is the ultimate divorce trigger and must be scored with a red flag.

Completing this task can also be an opportunity to re-evaluate your relationship, and to see what problems you consider to be capable of triggering a divorce.

Key Points

- Extramarital affairs and financial problems are the most common triggers of divorce.
- Divorce can be triggered either by a major sudden event, or by a combination of many small ongoing circumstances.

References & Suggested Reading

1. Crowe, M. (2005). *Overcoming relationship problems: A self-help guide using CBT*. London: Robinson.
2. Scarf, M. (1987). *Intimate Partners*. New York: Random House.
3. Papadopoulos, L. (2008). *What men say What woman hear.* Century.
4. Oberlin, L.H. (2005). *Surviving Separation and Divorce.* Adams Media, an F+ W Publication.
5. Wegscheider-Cruse, S. (1994). *Life after Divorce.* Health communications, Inc.

FIVE

The Divorce Emotional Reaction

"When a man points a finger at someone else, he should remember that three of his fingers are pointing at himself".
Anonymous

The Purpose

The purpose of this chapter is to evaluate your emotional reactions to divorce.

Introduction

Divorce is a highly emotional event and has a different affect on every member of the family.

In some marriages, the divorce is a product of a mutual decision made by both spouses to dissolve the marital ties, while in many other cases, the divorce is decided unilaterally, by only one spouse.

In the case of a unilateral decision to get a divorce, the spouse deciding to end the marriage is the Leaver or the Dumper, while the spouse passively waiting for the other spouse to start the process can be labelled as the Dumped.

During the divorce, both spouses experience a similar emotional reaction which often develops at the same time. However, the emotional reactions experienced by the Dumper can be slightly different from these emotions experienced by the Dumped. Sometimes, the Dumper's initial emotional response to the divorce process is a strong sense of relief, which quickly turns into guilt and shame. On the other hand, the most common initial emotional reaction of the dumped spouse is more of shock and stress. After the initial period, most of the emotional reactions are similar in both spouses.

The most common emotional responses to divorce are anxiety, depression, anger and guilt. The various emotional reactions can be experienced at a different intensity.

Any emotional reaction can develop any time during the divorce, resulting in a combination of anxiety and depressive symptoms that can easily be transformed into anger and back again to anxiety.

At times, feelings of anger can co-exist simultaneously with feelings of anxiety or depression. In fact, more commonly, there is a combination of several emotional states which co-exist simultaneously.

The divorce emotional reaction is normally felt by most people going through a divorce. However, the degree and intensity of each emotional state and the impact on the person's functionality can vary.

You should expect to have a different degree of emotional reaction during your divorce, which will invariably affect your life. The severity level of each emotional reaction can be measured in relation to its effect on your life, on your activities, and on your level of functioning.

The most common emotional reaction of divorcing people is illustrated in Table 5.1.

Figure 5.1: **The Divorce Emotional Reactions During the Disengagement**

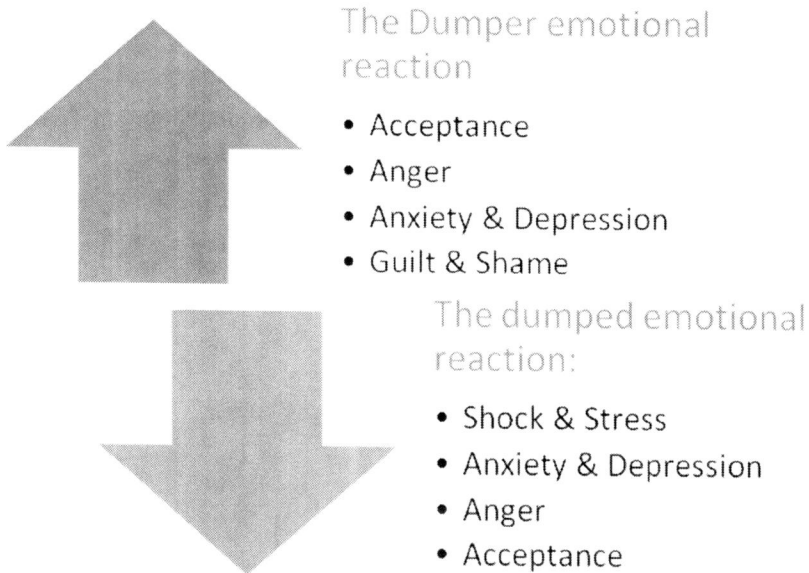

The Dumper emotional reaction

- Acceptance
- Anger
- Anxiety & Depression
- Guilt & Shame

The dumped emotional reaction:

- Shock & Stress
- Anxiety & Depression
- Anger
- Acceptance

The different emotional reactions will be extensively discussed in the next chapters.

Overview of the Disengagement Process

The disengagement process involves several periods which include a honeymoon period, a war period and a final truce period. Each disengagement period is linked to the various divorce-related events, as well as to the divorcing couple's emotional state.

During the honeymoon period, a predominant goodwill and positive intention is manifested which is very similar to the beginning of the relationship and marriage. Both spouses are motivated to keep the relationship positive, and are more willing to compromise in order to finish the divorce as quickly as possible, so that it will have a limited effect on the children. Unfortunately, the honeymoon period is usually a very short event, as personal interest and feelings of revenge often result in legal battles which are common to the war period.

The truce period is the final desirable stage which marks the end of the battle over the financial and custody issues, and the beginning of the new life phase.

In general, the move toward the truce period is the most desirable outcome of the divorce.

The relationship between the emotional reactions within the divorce periods is illustrated in Table 5.2.

Table 5.2   The Divorce Disengagement Process

The Dumper	E M O	5 Acceptance	D I V	The Truce Period
	T	4 Anger	O	The War Period
	I	3 Depression	R	
	O N	2 Anxiety	C E	The Honeymoon Period
	A	1 Guilt and Shame		
The Dumped	L	1 Shock & Stress	P E	The Honeymoon Period
	R	2 Anxiety	R	
	E A	3 Depression	I O	The War Period
	C	4 Anger	D	
	T I O N	5 Acceptance		The Truce Period

Each disengagement period is connected to the spouses' emotional states as well as to the divorce circumstances. Conflicts over financial issues or legal disputes over the management of the children can influence the speed with which each period resolves. The disengagement period progresses from the honeymoon to the truce period. Once the truce period is reached, it is highly unlikely that the relationship will slide back to an earlier period, unless there is a breach of a mutual consensus, or a breach of the signed legal agreement.

The ultimate goal of every successful divorce should be the ability to reach the truce period as quickly as possible.

The Honeymoon Period

The honeymoon period is the period that follows the beginning of the Divorce process. This period is usually brief and often lasts only as long as the guilt resulting from starting a divorce exists.

Unfortunately, as soon as the legal battle over the financial issues starts, the honeymoon period tends to evaporate.

During the honeymoon period, both spouses try to minimise their own stress levels by showing a more compromising attitude. The Dumper who often experiences feelings of shame and guilt will be more ready to compromise in order to ease his/her emotional pain, while the Dumped's state of shock also results in a more compromising attitude.

Unfortunately, the honeymoon period is commonly short. As soon as the shock and the guilt disappears, which usually corresponds with the onset of the legal battle, the war period commences.

Dr Shlomo Brook

The War Period

The war period is the period that most commonly follows the initial honeymoon phase. The war period is usually linked to the period in which each spouse is unwilling to compromise. The battlefield is the court room, while the legal advisors and the extended family act as the consultants.

The weapons used in the legal war are the sophisticated paperwork of the lawyers, and the manipulation manoeuvres made by both spouses.

Most commonly, the war period lasts until both sides reach an agreement regarding the finances and the custody issues.

During this period, feelings of anger coupled with an intransigent attitude are common.

Each spouse is motivated to gain as much as possible from the divorce. Sometimes, the need for revenge results in a strong desire to humiliate the ex-spouse. The frustration built over many years of unhappy marriage will finally be expressed and channelled via a legitimate legal outlet.

During the legal battle the stakes are high, and include the custody over your children, the visitation schedules, the house and the control of other family assets. In such a scenario, victory for you means that you will get as much as possible out of the marriage with the bonus of humiliating your ex-spouse.

The Final Stage: The Truce Period

The truce period is the period in which both spouses realise that continuing with the legal battle will cause more harm and pain and will adversely affect the children.

The truce period will start after the legal battle is over and both spouses are relatively satisfied with the agreement reached.

The truce period is the beginning of the new chapter in your life book and requires you to accept a new reality.

In the truce period, feelings of revenge can finally be replaced with acceptance, which will, in turn, finally lead to more positive goal-directed behaviour.

At which period is your divorce?

At the honeymoon period: Yes / No, Why do you think so: _____
_____

At the war period: Yes / No, Why do you think so: _____
_____

At the truce period: Yes / No, Why do you think so: _____
_____

Key Points

- The divorce can lead to serious emotional reactions.
- The emotional reactions are similar for both the Dumper and the Dumped.
- The divorce disengagement process proceeds through three periods: the honeymoon period, the war period and the truce period.

Suggested Reading

1. Oberlin, L.H. (2005). *Surviving Separation and Divorce*. Adams Media, an F+ W Publication.
2. Fisher, B., Alberti, R. (2006). *Rebuilding.* Impact Publishers inc.
3. Gadula, S.P. (2008). *Contemplating Divorce.* New Harbinger Publications, Inc.
3. Wegscheider-Cruse, S. (1994). *Life after Divorce.* Health communications, Inc.

SIX

Predicting Divorce Outcomes

"The past lies like a nightmare upon the present".
Karl Marx

The Purpose

The purpose of this chapter is to help you to identify the possible outcomes of your divorce.

Introduction

Predicting your divorce outcome is difficult and highly speculative, bearing some similarities to weather prediction. Divorce outcomes involve multiple variables which strongly influence the final results.

However, despite the inherent multiple variables that influence the outcome of your divorce, some factors have stronger effects on your divorce process than others, which might allow us a hazy glimpse into your future. Your past marital relationship is one of the strongest predictors of the nature of your divorce. Those who experienced reasonably good relationships with their ex-spouses during their marriages, will have a higher probability of a similar interaction style during the divorce, while stormy marital relationships will most probably result in a stormy divorce.

Your interpersonal interactions depend on your genetic makeup, and are further shaped by environmental factors. In other words, we were born with a predetermined capability to interact with our fellow humans which is further shaped by the significant figures in our lives who refine the way we relate to others.

Your first teachers are your parents and your siblings. Next in line are your peers and your school teachers with whom you interact daily, and so, by trial and error, you learn and develop your own interaction style.

Later in life you emulate those learned interactions with all the new people whom you meet. During adult life there is some room for improvement, and while learning new ways of interacting might prove difficult, existing techniques can still be modified.

Your marital interaction will proceed in a similar manner to the way you relate to others, and will most probably continue to shape your relationship style during your divorce.

In simple terms, it is more likely that having a past unhealthy interaction pattern with your spouse will continue and will most probably get worse during the divorce.

On the other hand, having experienced a positive past interactional style with your ex-spouse will not guarantee a positive relationship during the divorce. In addition, other factors such as legal and financial difficulties might further complicate and affect negatively a previously severed relationship.

Relying heavily on advice received from the legal team, as well as the abundant wisdom of friends and other relatives can further modify the divorce outcome.

This is illustrated in greater detail in Figure 6.1.

Figure 6.1   The Effect of Past Behaviour and External Factors on the Divorce Outcome

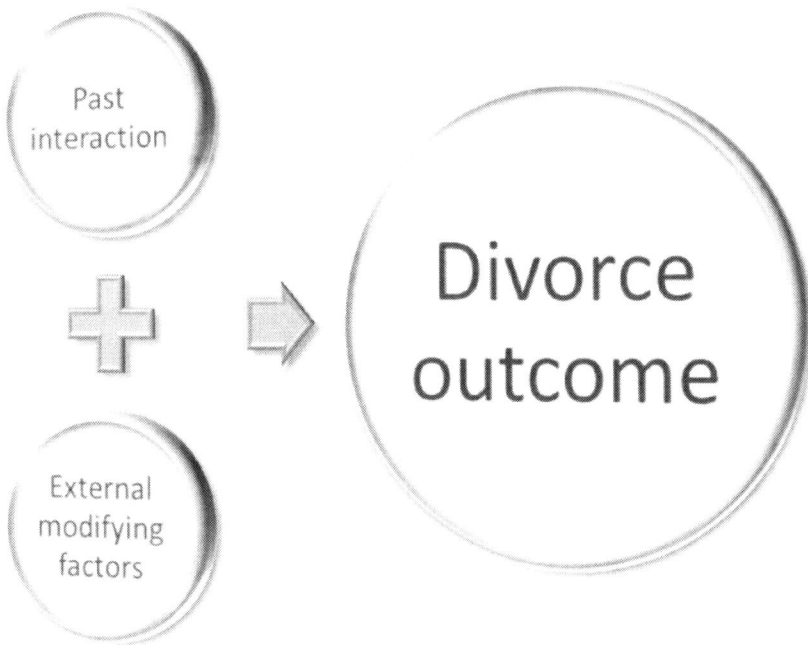

The Influence of the Past on the Future

As previously discussed, your past interactional style might give you some clues regarding the way you relate to others. In general, if you were capable of developing a warm and positive relationship with your ex-spouse, there is a higher probability that such a relationship will continue into your divorce.

Although in the divorce context, having a good marital relationship might sound misplaced and somewhat unreal as divorce is usually associated with conflicts and fights, it is nevertheless not uncommon to find a divorcing couple who experienced a positive relationship during their marriage, and are still able to maintain such an interactional style during and after the divorce. On the other hand, having a bad marriage with limited communication almost guarantees that future interactions will be conducted only by the legal teams.

Experiencing a good marital relationship implies an efficient communication pattern coupled with a high level of trust and mutual openness. Having such a marriage might suggest that you will be able to communicate efficiently with your ex-spouse, and that you will be able to share important information timeously, and will be able to share effectively the responsibilities required by raising your children.

On the other hand, a poor marriage will most likely predict confrontational divorce with limited probability to compromise over important issues. It is important to gain a better insight into your past interpersonal marital relationship in order to be able to predict your possible relationship with your ex-spouse during and after the divorce.

Completing Table 6.2 will help you to assess your past marital relationship according to six basic interactional parameters. All that you need to do is to tick the relevant box which best characterises your past relationship with your spouse.

Table 6.2.   Evaluating Your Past Marital Relationship

Past marital relationship parameters	Very good 5	Good 4	Okay 3	Bad 2	Very bad 1
Communication					
Level of trust & openness					
Level of flexibility & adaptation					

Level of intimacy & honesty					
Ability to share activities					
Conflict resolution abilities					
Total :					

A score of 0 – 10 implies a severely impaired past marital relationship. Your marriage had no communication which practically implies that you knew nothing about your spouse's needs, desires and dreams and *vice versa*. You were not able to solve your differences due to poor conflict resolution abilities. In addition, mutual trust during your marriage was more of a fantasy than a reality. In simple terms, your marriage looked bad and was bad.

A score of 11 – 20 implies that your marriage looked slightly better. You could maintain basic and limited communication with your spouse, and were able to share some necessary information, not because you wanted to, but because you had to. You were able to develop some sort of basic trust, although your conflict resolution skills required major and intense improvement. However, while generally your marriage looked okay, it still needed further improvement.

A score of 21 – 30 implies that your marriage was relatively good. You had a good level of communication and mutual trust. Your family activities were mutually decided upon, and were probably done together. Your marriage was good and looked good. The divorce is probably the result of a catastrophic event that ruined a near perfect marriage.

Table 6.3 summarises the different marital qualities.

Table 6.3   **Interpretation of the Quality of Your Marital Relationship**

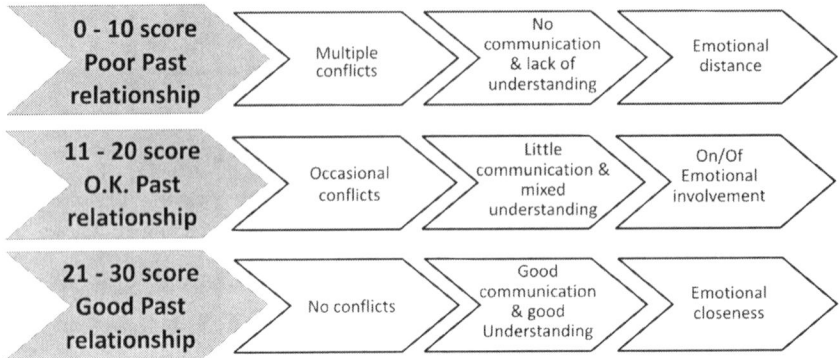

0 - 10 score Poor Past relationship	Multiple conflicts	No communication & lack of understanding	Emotional distance
11 - 20 score O.K. Past relationship	Occasional conflicts	Little communication & mixed understanding	On/Of Emotional involvement
21 - 30 score Good Past relationship	No conflicts	Good communication & good Understanding	Emotional closeness

In addition to an evaluation of your past marital interaction, looking at the influence of other people might change the course of your divorce. The following list is an example of who could possibly influence the outcome of your divorce:

- Family members
- Mutual friends
- Personal friends
- Therapist
- Personal coaches
- Legal advisors

Each person who knows you or your spouse either directly or indirectly can influence your divorce outcome. In general, the closer the contact you have with a given person, the higher the possibility that you may be influenced by him/her. Moreover, the higher you value the other person's views, the more influential s/he becomes. Complete Table 6.4 in order to evaluate who might affect you and how much influence they could have.

Table 6.4   The People and Their Effect on Your Divorce

The Person	Strong Effect	Moderate Effect	Minimal Effect
A. Family			
1			
2			
3			
4			
5			
B. Friends			
1			
2			
3			
4			
5			
C. Therapists			
1			
2			
3			
4			
5			
D. Legal Advisor			
1			
2			
3			

The Different Divorce Outcomes

Based on those factors you can now attempt to predict your divorce outcome. Table 6.5 includes several factors related to your marriage which might help you to extrapolate your own divorce.

Table 6.5   Your Predicted Divorce Outcome

	Good	**O. K**	**Bad**
Quality of past marital interaction	Good	O.K.	Impaired
The influence of others on you and on your spouse	None	Minimal	A lot
Presence of new obstacles	None	Minimal	A lot

Key Points

- The divorce outcome is variable.
- The divorce outcome depends on the past marital interpersonal interactional style and on the presence of ongoing life events and the affect of significant people on both spouses.
- The divorce can potentially have three different outcomes: A good outcome, a bad outcome, and a mixed bag outcome.

Suggested Reading

1.   Fisher, B., Alberti, R. (2005). Rebuilding: When your relationship ends. Impact publishers, inc.
2.   Gadoua, S.P. (2008). Contemplating divorce. New Harbinger Publications, Inc.
3.   Oberlin, L.H. (2000). Surviving Separation and Divorce. Adams Media: Avon.

SEVEN

Stress and Divorce

"When the going gets tough, the tough get going".
Anonymous

The Purpose

The purpose of this chapter is to explain the effects of the divorce-related stresses on you, on your family and on your life.

Introduction

Divorce is a serious event which has an overwhelming emotional and physiological impact on you and on your family.

In general, the early divorce period requires the most significant changes which will impact greatly on every aspect of your life. The unfolding divorce events produce unfamiliar situations which require major adapting skills.

Your previous ability to control your immediate environment will be strongly challenged by the divorce, which will often make you feel helpless, out of control and stressed. In general, the divorce will evict you and your spouse from your comfort zones, and will place both of you in unfamiliar territory.

Your new divorced life will look complex and overwhelming, and might make you feel confused, insecure and lonely with a desperate need for support and help.

You might feel that a short time out to pause for a few seconds might help you to control the chaos that fills your existence. Unfortunately this is not going to happen as your life continues relentlessly. Your work is waiting for you to continue to earn the much-needed income, and your children still have to continue with their busy schedules at school as well as with their after-school activities.

You will soon learn that your regular payments for your house and your car will relentlessly swallow your limited budget and will add to your many other worries.

I can almost hear you saying, "I can't do it anymore", "It's too much for me to handle". Headaches and a stiff neck will be a common daily experience along with the fine hand tremor which you might develop. Appointments and deadlines you have to meet will often be missed due to your reduced concentration and absent mind. You might feel as if have you reached a point at which you are not able to cope with life's pressures any more.

Experiencing these symptoms suggests that you are probably stressed.

So What is Stress?

Stress, in short, is the way your life pressure affects your body. Usually, stress is invariably associated with something bad. However, stress is not necessarily a bad or an undesirable phenomenon. Stress can also have a positive function. Stress will make you function at your best in order to face life's requirements.

Optimal levels of stress will mobilise your body's physical and psychological resources to optimise your functionality. Although having too much stress will overwhelm your body and exhaust its resources until you reach a total breakdown, life with no pressure would be unchallenging, and would prevent you from reaching your maximal potential. On the other hand, having too much pressure lasting for a long period of time will leave you in a state of complete burn-out and dysfunction.

The complex interaction between life stresses and your performance is illustrated in Figure 7.1. From this illustration you can see that low stress levels result in low performance, while too much stress results in a state of breakdown and limited functionality, and that the best performance is achieved only when stress is optimal.

Figure 7.1   The Relationship Between Stress and Performance

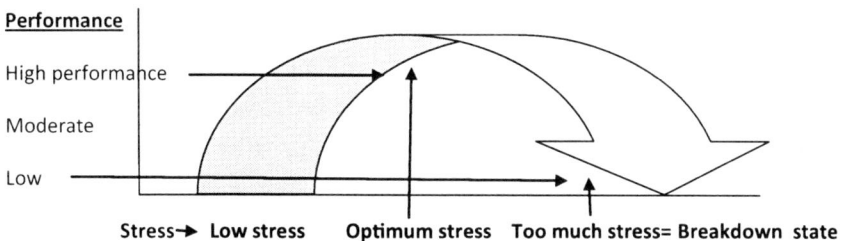

Every person can handle pressure. Some people are only able to function at their best when stress is extreme, while others are unable to manage even the tiniest pressure without becoming physically and emotionally sick.

In addition, the ability to handle pressure can change daily. On certain days you may be able to handle pressure easily, while on other days the same amount of pressure can be an overwhelming experience.

Your ability to handle stress is controlled by several brain sectors located in different parts of your brain. Each part plays a specific role in processing the external incoming information and generating a unique stress response.

How Your Brain Processes Life Pressure

The ability to process pressure is not exclusive to humans. Reaction to stress was always an indispensable element shared by all life forms. Existence depends greatly on the ability to recognise hostile environmental cues and to be able to generate an efficient response.

Since prehistoric times, humans dealt with an incredible amount of stress as was experienced by all creatures of those times. The stress in the ancient era was caused mainly as a result of the hostile environment and the constant need to look for food. The prehistoric environment was extremely dangerous for humans, as there were too many faster and stronger predators which were happy to hunt down the slow and weak early humans and include them on their daily menu.

These innate physical disadvantages created the need to develop an efficient alarm system which enabled the humans to survive in hostile territory. The prehistoric stress was relatively simple and limited. Either you could find food, or you would die from hunger. Either you could develop survival skills to face the harsh weather, or you would die from extreme cold or heat. Survival required an optimal level of functioning at any given moment with no room for mistakes.

Survival required an efficient built-in alarm system which was able to recognise hostile environmental signals and was capable of generating an adequate, efficient, automatic and fast response. Only the strongest, the fastest and the fittest animals could survive.

Over the centuries, life on earth changed dramatically. The human race became the strongest, dominating all other animals and became capable of manipulating the environment.

Such changes required less reliance on an effective alarm system needed for survival. Unfortunately, the downgrading to an alarm system to match the modern environmental stresses was not carried out due to its massive importance for survival.

Modern stresses are significantly different from those experienced by our ancestors. Today, food is hunted in air-conditioned departmental stores and comes wrapped in plastic, while the extreme weather conditions are better controlled by efficient air-conditioners.

Driving to work does not require you to have any special skill to help you face a dangerous predator other than another fellow human driver. However, despite these massive technological advances, there is still a huge amount of pressure which you need to face. Modern day stress involves complex social circumstances and growing financial needs in an environment where fewer jobs are available.

Nevertheless, modern stress has limited immediate danger to human life. Today, stress is more like a chronic pressure which has a gradual deteriorating impact on your ability to cope with it. In such circumstances, having the ancient built-in super alarm system is equivalent to having a super-modern engine placed in an ancient model of car. The result of such a mismatch is often catastrophic. Having a super stress-buster alarm system which operates under our modern day pressure can result in a constant state of overdrive and severe physical and psychological reactions.

Where is the Alarm System Located?

The alarm system is located in several interconnected brain areas specialised to handle external pressure. Once the danger signal is captured by your sensory system, an electrical signal travels through your brain to those specialised alarm sites, and will activate, mobilising your body's resources in order to meet potential dangers and safeguard your life.

Your initial reaction to danger can either be confrontational or a quick disengagement. Such reactions to danger were initially described in 1932 by Walter Canon who investigated animals' physiological responses to stress. When Canon confronted laboratory cats with dogs, he discovered that both animals responded with either a readiness to fight, or by running away from the scene. Canon termed these animal reactions the 'fight or flight' response.

Over the years our understanding of the alarm system has evolved considerably. Each site once activated is able to either suppress or to generate a reaction. The complex stress buster sites and their principal duties are illustrated in Figure 7.2.

Fig. 7.2:   The Alarm System Stress Management Sites

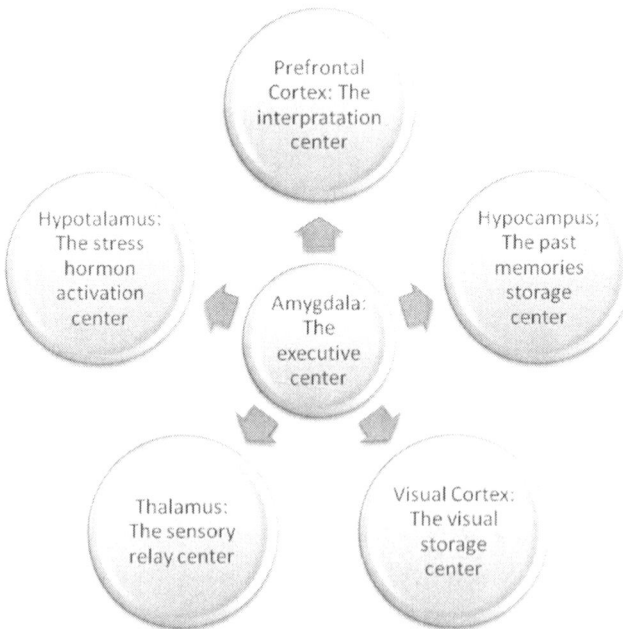

How the Alarm System Works

The alarm system's response is automatically activated by stress. Each noxious external stimulus is capable of activating the alarm system. The danger stimulus gets transmitted to a sensory relay station called the *Thalamus*. The *thalamu*s acts as a sensory relay station transferring incoming data to *the visual cortex* which is located in the posterior part of the brain and is responsible for processing the visual information and identifying its content. Once the stimulus is identified, the *visual cortex* alerts another site called *the hippocampus*, which stores memories of previous threats. The *hippocampus* matches the new event with similar stored past events. In the case of a positive match, the *hippocampus* rapidly alerts the executive site called the *amygdale* which is responsible for generating a physiological response. In addition, there is a parallel reaction which occurs simultaneously at another brain site located in *the prefrontal cortex. The prefrontal cortex* logically evaluates the same noxious stimulus and either allows the *amygdala* to go ahead and activate the body's physiological response or to refrain from action. This complicated alarm system action is summarised in Figure 7.3.

Fig. 7.3: **How the Alarm System Works**

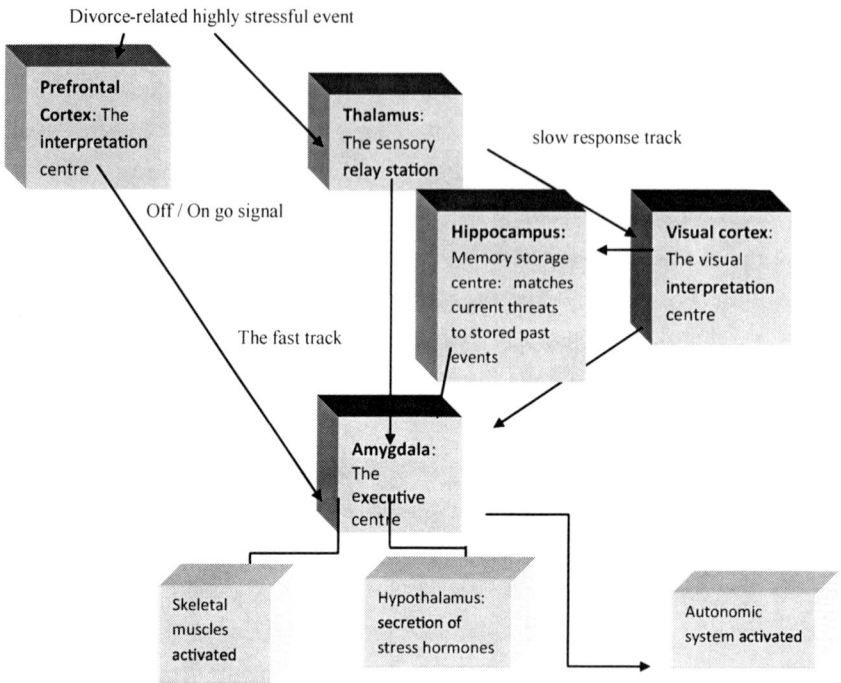

Divorce-related highly stressful event

Prefrontal Cortex: The interpretation centre

Thalamus: The sensory relay station

slow response track

Off / On go signal

Hippocampus: Memory storage centre: matches current threats to stored past events

Visual cortex: The visual interpretation centre

The fast track

Amygdala: The executive centre

Skeletal muscles activated

Hypothalamus: secretion of stress hormones

Autonomic system activated

What Happens When the Stress System is Activated?

The activation of the alarm system results in a physiological response which will affect your muscles, your stress hormones and your autonomic nervous system, and will allow your body to prepare and to react to any external stress.

Cortisol – The Principal Stress Hormone, How and Where is it Made?

Cortisol is your principal stress hormone. Cortisol is produced by your kidneys and from there it travels via your blood and spreads all over your body.

The production of Cortisol is regulated by your brain via a complicated process. Its starts with the *amygdala* which stimulates a specific brain circuit called the *Hypothalamic-Pituitary-Adrenal* axis, which is shortly named the HPA axis. The HPA axis consists of three distinctive sites of which two are located in the brain and the third is located in the upper part of your kidneys. In the brain's site, the HPA system includes the *hypothalamus* and the *pituitary gland*, while in the kidney the HPA system includes the external part of the kidney called the *adrenal cortex*. The HPA axis controls and regulates the rates of Cortisol production and its release to the blood stream.

The overall control of the HPA activities is regulated by the *amygdala*, the *hypocampus* and by the inhibitory effects of the circulating Cortisol levels.

The activation of the HPA system produces a hormone called Cortico Release Hormone (CRH) which travels in the brain to *the pituitary gland* where it activates the release of another stress hormone called ACTH. The ACTH, once released to the bloodstream will travel to the kidneys where it activates the production and the release of Cortisol, the principal stress hormone.

Are you confused? Me too! However, with a little bit of imagination this complex mechanism can be simplified, hopefully by Figure 7.4.

Fig. 7.4   The HPA Axis: The Production of the Stress Hormone

Amygdala & Hippocampus (modulating function)

activates   **blocks**

+   -

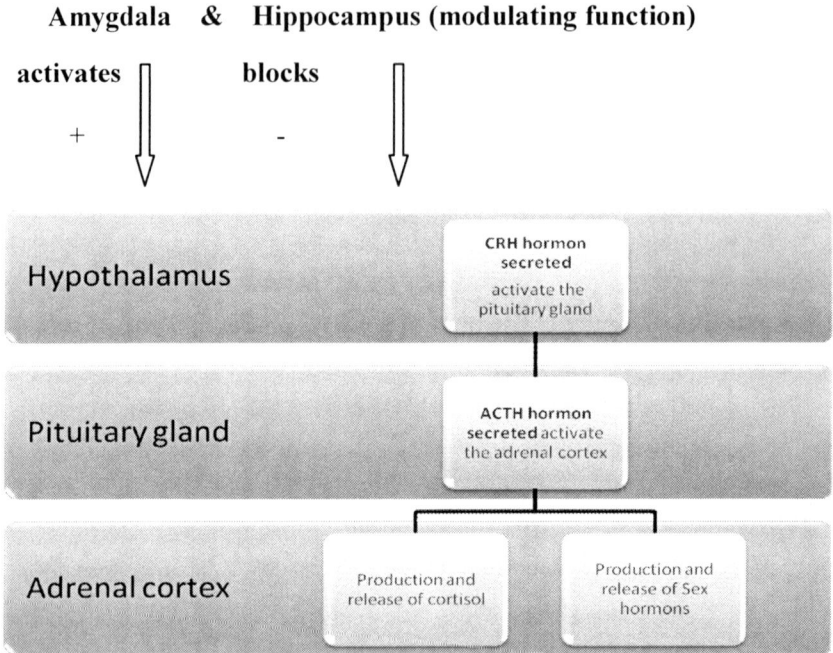

Hypothalamus	CRH hormon secreted — activate the pituitary gland
Pituitary gland	ACTH hormon secreted activate the adrenal cortex
Adrenal cortex	Production and release of cortisol	Production and release of Sex hormons

The end result of having stress will be a drastic increase in your Cortisol blood levels which can help you to face your stresses.

How the Cortisol works

The Cortisol regulates and mobilises your body's energy resources by raising your body's available energy via its effects on your fat tissue, your liver and your muscles.

In the fat tissue, Cortisol activates the release of fatty acids via a process called Lipolysis. The fatty acids released from your fat tissue are an important source of energy as they can be transformed into sugar by your liver.

In the liver, Cortisol is responsible for the release of sugar to the bloodstream in a process called Glycolysis.

In the muscle tissue, Cortisol is responsible for the release of amino acids and their conversion to energy in a process performed by the liver called Gluconeogenesis.

The various effects of Cortisol on energy production are summarised in Figure 7.5.

Fig. 7.5   How Cortisol Affects Your Body's Energy Resources

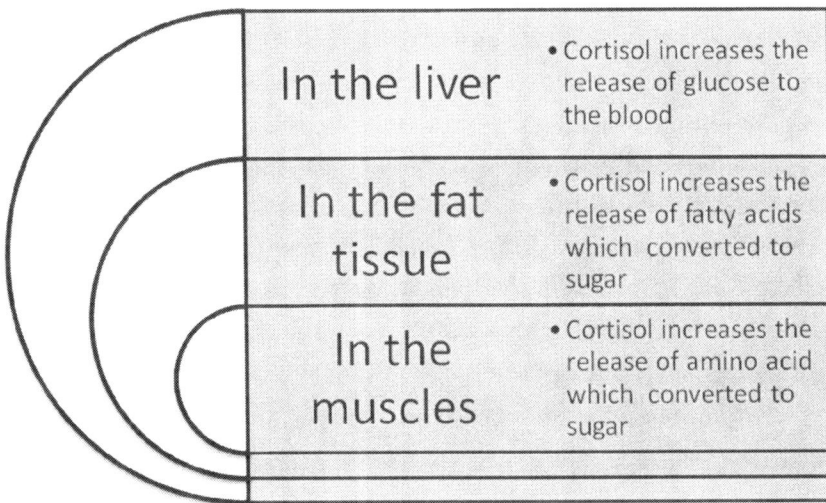

In the liver	• Cortisol increases the release of glucose to the blood
In the fat tissue	• Cortisol increases the release of fatty acids which converted to sugar
In the muscles	• Cortisol increases the release of amino acid which converted to sugar

Cortisol activity is not, however exclusive to your body's energy resources management. While Cortisol increases your body's access to its energy resources, it also temporarily suppresses your immune system, your body's growth ability and your body's digestive system. Such temporary suppression of these other bodily functions is aimed at saving energy on less important bodily functions.

Having excessive Cortisol levels circulating over a long period of time can have a deleterious effect on your body. High levels of Cortisol eventually deplete your body muscle mass, and reduce your body bone density. In addition, prolonged high Cortisol levels can also cause an increase in your blood sugar levels which can lead to a condition called Type Two Diabetes. Another problem associated with high Cortisol levels is increased blood-pressure. The suppressive effects of high Cortisol levels on your immunological system can lead to an increased sensitivity to contract infections. Another unwanted effect of high Cortisol levels is its negative effect on your memory, concentration, and on your moods, which can lead to depression and to severe concentration impairment. In a normal condition the secretion of Cortisol has a daily circadian rhythm. The highest cortisone levels measured in your blood are between 6 a.m. and 8 a.m. The purpose of having the high level of Cortisol during the early morning hours is to help your body to get up and prepare itself for the upcoming daily requirements. After your body has experienced a morning surge of Cortisol, its blood levels reduce during the day to reach its lowest level between 12 a.m. and 2 a.m., the time when your body is supposed to be resting free of stress. In addition to the normal regular daily variation in Cortisol blood levels, your diet and your emotional state can also influence Cortisol levels. The Cortisol secretion can be increased by high consumption of caffeine, as well as by anxiety and depression and by physical activity.

So is Cortisol Good or Bad for You?

By now you are probably feeling slightly overwhelmed and confused by this huge amount of information. As you have probably gathered from the information so far, Cortisol has multiple functions, some of which are beneficial, while others can be harmful to you. In addition to stress, anxiety and depression can also increase your Cortisol levels in your blood, placing additional strain on your body.

In general, persistent and prolonged high Cortisol blood levels can cause many health problems which are summarised in Table 7.6.

Table 7.6:   The Negative Effects of Cortisol on Your Body

The target system & organs	The clinical effects
The cardio-vascular effects	Hypertension, increase in blood tryglicerids and cholesterol levels
The metabolic effects	Increase in the blood glucose levels leading to insulin resistance, and also responsible for metabolic syndrome
The mineral effects	Loss of calcium from the bones which can lead to Osteoporosis.
The effects on the sex drive	Reduces sex hormone levels & reduces sex drive
The immunological effects	Reduces immunity reaction which can lead to increased sensitivity to infections
The effects on the brain	Brain atrophy, impaired memory, dementia

Overall, stress has a mixed effect on your body, and there is a wide consensus that prolonged enduring pressure is counterproductive and hazardous to your health.

Key Points

•   Divorce is one of the most highly stressful life events.

- Stress activates a complicated alarm system which resides in the pre-frontal cortex and the limbic system.
- Cortisol is the principal stress hormone which has various metabolic effects.

References

1. Cannon, W.B. (1932). *The wisdom of the body*. New York: Norton.
2. Selye, H. (1974). *Stress without distress*. New York: Lippincott.
3. Holmes, T. & Rahe, R. (1967). The social readjustment rating scale. *Journal of Psychosomatic Research*, 11: 213 – 218.
4. Lewin, K. (1935). *A dynamic theory of personality*. New York: Mcgraw-Hill.
5. Lazarus, R. & Folkman, S. (1984). *Stress, Appraisal and Coping*. New York: Springer.
6. Rotter, J.B. (1982). *The development and application of social learning theory*. New York: Praeger.

Suggested Reading

1. Talbott, S.M. (2002). *The Cortisol Connection*. Hunter House Inc.
2. Charlesworth, E.A and Nathan, R.G. (1984). *Stress management*. Ballantine books.
3. Brewer, S. (1999). *The Ultimate Stress Buster*. London: Ebury Press.
4. Powell, T. (2000). *Stress Free Living*. DK Publishing, inc.

EIGHT

Your Divorce Stress

"One filled with joy preaches without preaching".
Mother Teresa of Calcutta

How Does Your Body Handle Stress?

The stress management alarm apparatus is a highly effective system which is universally installed in most animal brains and which aims at self-preservation and adaptation to environmental threats.

The differences between a human alarm system and that of most animals hinges on its additional ability to be controlled by the prefrontal cortex, a brain area located in the upper frontal part of your brain which has the additional capacity to evaluate each external situation and to determine its potential for danger.

Modern day stress is more commonly provoked by social context, rather than by life and death situations. According to Hans Selye, humans are capable of adapting to stress in a specific manner which he termed the General Adaptation Syndrome, or GAS for short.

The General Adaptation Syndrome – GAS:

The General Adaptation Syndrome is a term created by Hans Seyle to describe the way people adapt to stress. According to Seyle, the stress adaptation process proceeds along three phases which include the alarm phase, the resistance stage and the exhaustion stage.

A. **The alarm phase**

The alarm phase activates your initial response to stress. During the alarm phase, your body reacts to stress by increasing your heart rate in order to pump more blood to your brain and to your muscles. The hyperventilation will supply more oxygen to your vital organs, while your liver will make more sugar available to meet the required energy needs. Your blood clotting time will become shorter in order to allow less bleeding in case of an injury, while your digestive system activities will reduce to a minimum. This whole process will occur in seconds in order to be able to face any external challenge and to prepare you for a fight, or for flight.

B. **The Resistance stage**

Suffering prolonged stress requires a long-term optimal response. The resistance stage is the period in which your body reaches its optimal response to the stressful situation and you function at your highest potential in order to handle stress in the most efficient way.

C. **The exhaustion stage**

Your body resources are not, however, unlimited. As time goes by, you will need to utilise your energy for other body functions. Undergoing continuous stress will eventually exhaust all of your body's energy resources and will lead to a state of exhaustion and eventual collapse.

The GAS reaction is illustrated in Fig 8.1.

Fig. 8.1   The GAS Reaction (Adapted from Seyle)

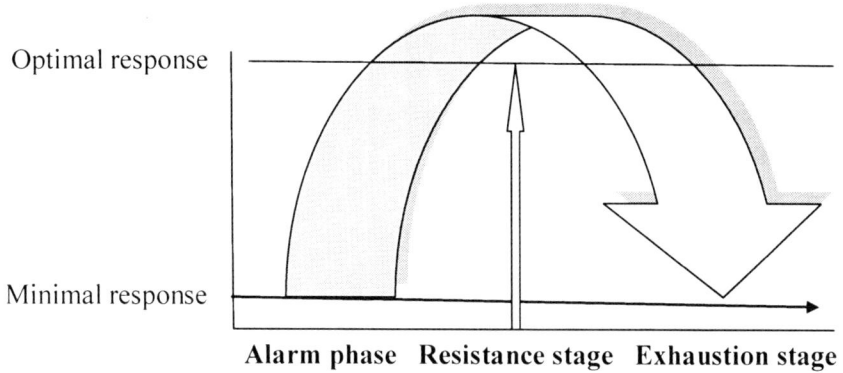

Optimal response

Minimal response

Alarm phase   Resistance stage   Exhaustion stage

As you can see some levels of stress are important for optimal functionality while too much stress for an extended period is hazardous to your health and can lead to a metabolic and a mental breakdown.

What are Life Stresses?

Life stresses can be divided into three categories based on their psychological impact.
*   Minimally stressful life events
*   Moderately stressful life events
*   Severely stressful life events

Minimally Stressful Life Events

Minimal life stresses are the daily minor hassles you regularly face during your normal day-to-day activities. Daily hassles are hardly noticeable and require minimal attention. Although separately, daily hassles have limited impact, when they accumulate they are capable of triggering your alarm response. Examples of daily hassles include paying the household bills, standing in long queues, being stuck in the traffic, or attending to a frustrating customer in a busy shop.

Moderately Stressful Life Events

Moderate life stresses are created by circumstances which have a stronger impact and require a vigorous adaptive response. Moderately stressful life events will activate your alarm system easily. Examples of moderately stressful life events include losing your wallet, or having a minor car accident. Both events are not life-threatening, yet they can be highly upsetting. Moderately stressful events require intense attention and substantial energy invested in their resolution. The motor vehicle accident requires you to notify the local police and your insurance company, as well as to make a costly visit to the panel beater. Those actions are time-consuming, irritating and highly inconvenient and will cause worry and stress.

Severely Stressful Life Events

Severe stresses are, fortunately, much less frequent, yet, once they occur, they are usually highly disturbing. Examples of severely stressful life events are the death of a loved one and divorce. Major stressful life events require your maximal adaptation and coping skills. The common factor underlying most major stressful life events is a loss. Divorce involves multiple losses, and can include financial loss, loss of friends, loss of your extended family and sometimes the loss of your children. Major life events either pose a direct threat to your life or to your personal wellbeing.

The Social Readjustment Rating Scale

The social readjustment rating scale was developed by Holmes & Rahe in order to evaluate the effects of stressful life events on one's life. Each life event is assigned a specific score based on its stressful impact. The death of a spouse and undergoing a divorce are the events with the highest scores, while going on vacation scores the lowest. According to Holmes, life events can have a cumulative effect on your health and can lead to health problems.

Table 8.2   **The Social Readjustment Rating Scale [Modified]**

Life event	Mean score
Death of spouse	100
Divorce	73
Marital separation	65
Prison sentence	63
Death of a close family member	63
Personal illness	53
Marriage	50
Termination of employment	47

Marital reconciliation	45
Retirement	45
Change of residence	20
Change in social activities	18
Vacation	13
Christmas	12
Minor violation of the law	11

The ability to predict and to master forthcoming events can drastically influence their ability to cause stress. While unpredictable and uncontrollable events will be experienced as more stressful, a predicted event can allow adequate time for one to prepare and to take counter measures that might influence and reduce the impact of that event. In addition, the values attributed to each event will significantly influence its stressful impact. Pursuant to the value attributed to each life event, a minor event can be experienced as highly stressful if it is perceived as highly important.

What are Your Stress-Provoking Life Circumstances?

Table 8.3 will enable you to assess your life circumstances and their impact. You are required to score each event based on its perceived impact on you and on your family.

Table 8.3   Your Life Stresses

Your Daily Hassels	No Impact = 1	Moderate Impact = 2	High Impact = 3
1			
2			
3			
4			
5			
6			
7			
8			
9			
10			
Your Moderate Stresses			
1			
2			
3			
4			
5			
Your Major Stresses			
1			
2			
3			
4			
5			
Total Score			

What are Your Most Common Divorce-Related Stresses?

Divorce is one of the most stressful life events. It has the highest score on the social readjustment rating scale, and can impact significantly on your physical and your emotional wellbeing. Table 8.4 contains several examples of various divorce-related circumstances. Score any event which is relevant to your situation based on its perceived impact on you and on your family.

Table 8.4   Divorce Related Stresses Impact score

1	2	3	4	5	6	7	8	9	10
No Im-pact		Mild Im-pact		Moder-ate Im-pact		Se-vere Im-pact			Ex-treme Im-pact

Divorce-related event	Impact score	Divorce-related event	Impact score
You feel lonely		Your alcohol con-sumption has in-creased	
Your new family situation has little harmony		Difficulty managing your new family re-quirements	
The never-ending conflict with your ex-spouse		Difficulty managing your new household chores	
The poor commu-nication with your ex-spouse		Difficulty dealing with the legal battle	
The increased re-sponsibilities		Difficulty managing your children's lives	
The reduced social life		Difficulty managing your finances	
The lack of trust in your ex-spouse		Difficulty coping with work-related pressure	
The reduction in your leisure activi-ties		Managing housing issues	

Difficulties in managing your children's problems		Difficulty managing your children's school activities	
Difficulty managing the involvement of your friends and colleagues in your life		Difficulty gaining your family's acceptance of a new lover	

The higher your perceived impact score, the higher your stress will be.

In addition to life events, divorce-related stress can also develop from the following sources:

- Frustration
- Conflicts
- Pressure

Frustration

Frustration develops in a situation in which the pursuit towards achieving a specific goal is blocked. In other words, you feel frustrated whenever you want something and are unable to get it. Unfortunately, frustration is a common event which tends to happen all the time. You become frustrated when the book you ordered did not arrive when you expected it, or you may become frustrated whenever you are stuck in traffic and arrive late at your destination. Frustration can be a transient feeling which is easily controlled, while at times, however, especially during the divorce, there can be many events which may make you feel frustrated and stressed.

The divorce-related losses are particularly problematic as they deprive you of things you used to have during your marriage. For example, losing your spouse to another lover can be minimally frustrating, while losing your children in the divorce settlement can be extremely frustrating and highly stressful. Similarly, losing your previous lifestyle can be particularly frustrating.

Completing Table 8.5 will help you assess your frustration levels.

Table 8.5   Frustration Impact Score

1	2	3	4	5	6	7	8	9	10
No Im-pact		Mild Im-pact		Moder-ate Im-pact		Se-vere Im-pact			Ex-treme Im-pact

Frustrating incident	Impact score	Frustrating incident	Impact score
1.		5.	
2.		6.	
3.		7.	
4.		8.	

The higher the frustration impact score, the higher your stress will become.

Conflicts

Conflicts develop whenever people with different motivations compete for their fulfilment. According to Kurt Lewin, there are three types of personal conflicts.

- **The approach – approach conflict**
- **The avoidance – avoidance conflict**
- **The approach – avoidance conflict**

The Approach-Approach Conflict:

The approach-approach conflict develops due to the need to choose between *two attractive goals*. An example of such conflict is when you have to choose between two or more new plasma TV sets in an appliance store. When you choose one option this automatically implies that the other option will be lost. Such an internal conflict type involves loss. However, the overall outcome of such conflict has a limited impact on your life and is mildly stressful. In contrast, whenever you need to fulfil a bigger need or an important life goal then such conflict's stress impact will be much higher. An example of divorce-related approach-approach conflict is when you need to choose between the beach house you recently acquired and the boat lying idly at the quayside.

The Avoidance-Avoidance Conflict.

The avoidance-avoidance conflict develops when a choice must be made between *two unattractive goals,* that is, you must choose between two repellent options. An example of divorce-related approach avoidance-avoidance conflict is when you need to choose between your city house located in a bad neighbourhood and the beach house which you recently took out a huge bond to acquire. As you can see, neither of the choices is attractive, thus this choice involves a fair amount of stress.

Dr Shlomo Brook

The approach-Avoidance Conflict.

The approach-avoidance conflict develops when a choice must be made between *two attractive and unattractive aspects*. An example of divorce-related approach-avoidance conflict is when you need to choose between keeping your family car or the house which you recently acquired which you know will be difficult to maintain. The divorce represents the perfect arena for interpersonal conflict to develop. Each spouse has different needs and goals to fulfil which are often opposite. In such circumstances, the divorce can create unlimited conflicts. Interpersonal conflicts either involve material issues such as how to split the family assets, while other interpersonal conflicts involve abstract issues such as how to manage the children.

Complete Table 8.6 in order to evaluate your most prominent conflicting issues and their relative impact on you.

Table 8.6   Conflicts Impact Score

1	2	3	4	5	6	7	8	9	10
No Impact		Mild Impact		Moderate Impact		Severe Impact			Extreme Impact

Personal conflicts	Impact score	Impersonal conflicts	Impact score
1.		5.	
2.		6.	
3.		7.	
4.		8.	

The higher the conflicts impact score you get, the higher your stress is.

Pressure

Pressure develops when you are expected to behave in a certain way. For example, a university worker is expected to publish in leading journals in order to be able to maintain his position and status. Similarly, pressure mounts after you get divorced, as you are expected to be the perfect parent even though the circumstances become much less favourable. As a divorced parent your income is much lower, and the help needed to raise the children is less, yet you are still expected to maintain the same lifestyle and equally, to be able to cope with your children's needs. Completing Table 8.7 will enable you to assess the amount of pressure you have in your life.

Table 8.7   Pressure Impact Score

1	2	3	4	5	6	7	8	9	10
No Impact		Mild Impact		Moderate Impact		Severe Impact			Extreme Impact

Pressure	Impact score	Pressure	Impact score
1.		5.	
2.		6.	
3.		7.	
4.		8.	

Again, the higher the pressure impact score, the higher your stress becomes.

Your total stress levels depend on a combination of the various life events, coupled with the amount of conflicts you experience during and after the divorce, and the amount of frustration and pressure that you're experiencing daily. The more highly stressed you feel, the higher the probability that you will develop stress-related physical and psychological symptoms which will be explained further in the following section.

What are the Physical Stress-Related Manifestations?

Excessive and persistent stress, will, eventually, generate physical and psychological symptoms. The physical symptoms of stress can be experienced daily with a varying degree of intensity. Some days you might feel crippled by a specific symptom, while on another day you might function as if nothing bothers you. The physical stress related symptoms are illustrated in Figure 8.8.

Figure 8.8   Stress Related Physical Symptoms

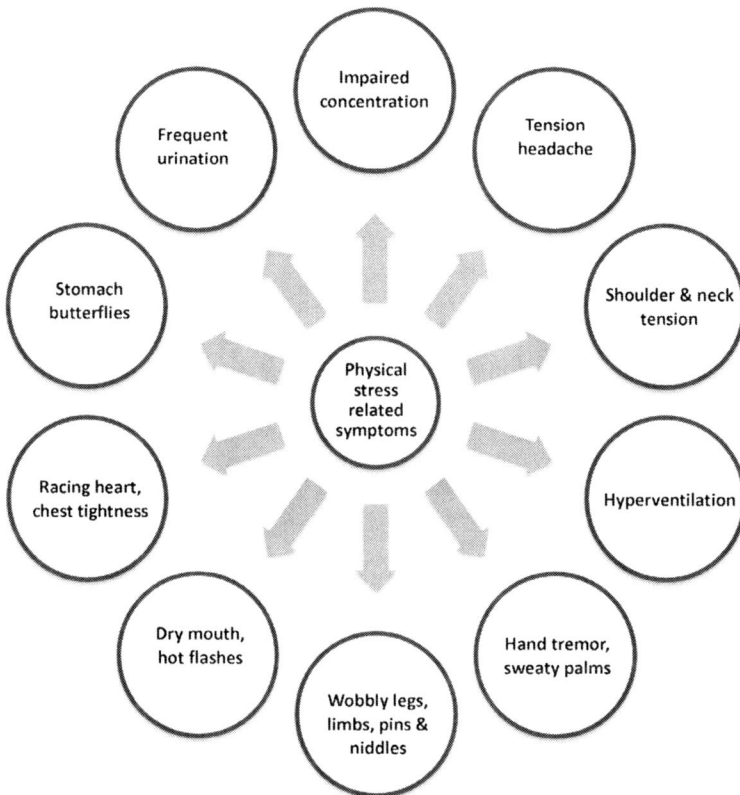

The stress-related physical symptoms can be highly disturbing and can severely affect your life, while the mild physical symptoms can go unnoticed despite their daily presence, and will require little effort to manage them, other symptoms can be severe and may require intense treatment.

Headaches, for example, are one of the most common stress-related physical symptoms. Despite the unpleasant presence of a headache, its impact on your daily functioning can be minimal on some days, while it can be severely debilitating on others. Heartburn is another example of a stress-related physical symptom which can be experienced daily. Heartburn can often be managed successfully with over-the-counter medication, while in some instances persistent heartburn can lead to duodenal ulcers. In general, it is highly important to treat not only the actual physical conditions, but also their causes.

Completing Table 8.9 will allow you to evaluate your stress-related physical symptoms and assess their impact on your life. Each symptom should be evaluated according to its frequency and its impact on your daily functioning. Remember that your evaluation is totally subjective.

Table 8.9   Score Your Stress-Related Physical Symptoms in X and Their Impact on Your Daily Activities in Y

Stress symptom	No symptom	Occa-sional presence	Daily present	Mild impact	Mod-erate impact	Severe impact
	X = 0	X = 1	X=2	Y = 1	Y = 2	Y = 3
You ex-perience reduced concen-tration						

You experience tension headaches					
You experience a dry mouth					
You experience neck & shoulder tension					
You experience a racing heart					
You experience chest tightness					
You experience hyperventilation					
You experience trembling hands					

You experi- ence a frequent need to urinate						
You ex- perience excessive sweating						
You ex- perience digestive problems						
Total score						

The amount of physical symptoms and their impact on your life is measured by adding the various scores.

Your total score	Total Score	Score interpretation
	0 – 18	You have Mild stress-related physical symptoms with a mild impact on your life
	19 – 36	You have Moderate stress-related physical symptoms with a moderate impact on your life
	37 – 55	You have Severe stress-related physical symp- toms with a severe impact on your life

In addition to having physical symptoms, stress can also cause severe emotional reactions. The most common stress-related emotional symptoms are tension, anxiety, depressive moods, irritability, guilt and anger. Each of those stress-related emotional reactions will be covered separately in the following chapters.

In addition to the physical and the emotional reactions, stress can also cause behavioural symptoms. The most common behavioural manifestations of stress include cynicism, resentment, animosity, over-sensitivity and defensive behaviour. Having maladaptive behaviour can lead to multiple conflicts which, in turn, can increase stress levels with their accompanying physical and emotional reactions.

Completing Table 8.10 will help you to identify the most common areas of your stress.

Table 8.10   Your Overall Stress Levels

	None/ Low	Few/ Moderate	A lot/ High
Amount of life events			
Amount of conflicts			
Amount of frustrations			
Amount of pressure			
Amount of physical symptoms			
Amount of emotional symptoms			
Amount of behavioural symptoms			

Overall stress levels	

Key Points

- A divorce is one of the most highly stressful life events.
- Stress creates multiple physical, emotional and behavioural symptoms.
- GAS is the way your body responds to stress.

• Stress can develop from minor and major life events as well as from pressure, frustration and conflicts.

References

1. Cannon, W.B. (1932). *The wisdom of the body.* New York: Norton.
2. Selye, H. (1974). *Stress without distress.* New York: Lippincott.
3. Holmes, T & Rahe, R. (1967). The social readjustment rating scale. *Journal of Psychosomatic Research,* 11: 213 – 218.
4. Lewin, K. (1935). *A dynamic theory of personality.* New York: Mcgraw-Hill.
5. Lazarus, R & Folkman, S. (1984). *Stress, Appraisal and Coping.* New York: Springer.
6. Rotter, J.B. (1982). *The development and application of social learning theory.* New York: Praeger.

Suggested Reading

1. Talbott, S.M. (2002). *The Cortisol Connection.* Hunter House Inc.
2. Charlesworth, E.A and Nathan, R.G. (1984). *Stress management.* Ballantine books.
3. Brewer, S. (1999). *The Ultimate Stress Buster.* London: Ebury Press.
4. Powell, T. (2000). *Stress Free Living.* DK Publishing, inc.

NINE

Divorce Stress Management

"Science is the great antidote to the poison
of enthusiasm and superstition".
Adam Smith, Wealth of Nations, 1776

The Purpose

The purpose of this chapter is to evaluate how you can handle your stresses and their related symptoms.

How do You Cope with Your Divorce Stress?

In the previous chapter you learned that moderate levels of stress are essential in order for you to function at your best, however an excessive amount of stress will have the opposite effect, and will cause serious physiological and psychological problems. Divorce is extremely stressful and is often associated with severe health and psychological problems.

Your ability to handle stress relies on the coping mechanisms you acquire over the years from the significant figures you come in contact with.

Coping mechanisms are *conscious processes* that operate within your mental awareness which enable you to adopt the right strategy in order to be able to face your stress. The principal aim of all the deployed coping strategies is to maintain your daily functioning at the highest possible levels. In other words, your coping strategies will help you to face the stressful divorce circumstances adequately, and will enable you to handle these in a constructive and productive manner.

Coping strategies can be highly effective in reducing stress, if deployed correctly however, your coping strategies tend to focus on the problem rather than on the cause of it. According to Lazarus, there are two types of coping mechanisms:

•   Positive coping strategies
•   Negative coping strategies

The Positive Coping Strategies

The positive coping strategies are those activities you do which can help you to handle the divorce-related stress efficiently.

Table 9.1 summarises the characteristics of the principal positive coping strategies:

Table 9.1   The Positive Coping Strategies

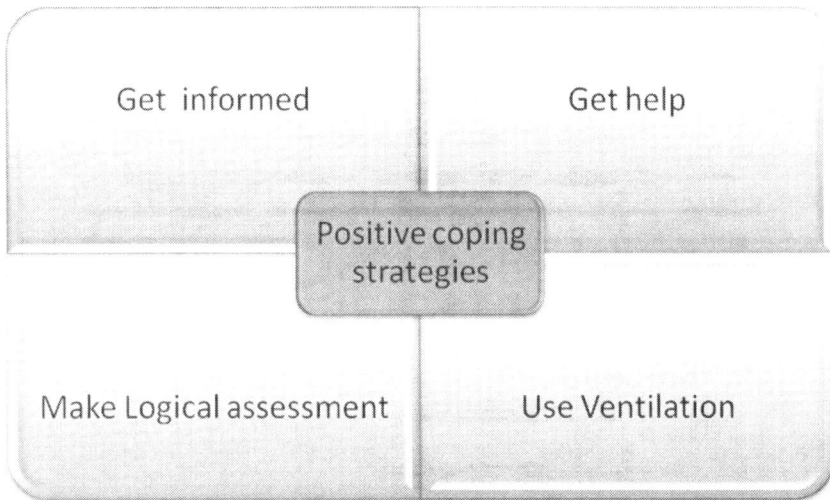

Get informed	Get help
Make Logical assessment	Use Ventilation

Positive coping strategies

- *Get information* – **Being** informed is one of the most important positive divorce coping strategies at your disposal. Gathering as much information as possible from any reliable source will allow you to plan your next move. Information is power, and having the right information at the right time enables you to calculate your next step timeously and to gain some control over the situation. Needless to say, a lack of control is highly stressful.
- *Get help from others* – Getting help is a highly important coping skill which requires you to be able to reach out and get emotional and practical support from significant others. The bigger and more reliable your support network is, the better your ability to master difficult situations during your divorce.
- *Ventilation of negative emotions* – Ventilation is an important coping skill that allows you to express your negative emotions to a supportive listener in a controlled manner.
- *Logical assessment of the situation*: Logic is one of the most

important tools available to you. During the divorce you need to assess each situation logically, and weigh up your available options in order to make the best decisions and to plan your future steps.

On the other hand, there are several other coping strategies which, when employed result in a negative impact on your life. Instead of reducing stress, these negative coping skills rather increase your stress levels. The characteristics of these negative coping strategies are their inability to reduce your stress.

Table 9.2 summarises the most common negative divorce-related coping strategies.

Table 9.2   The Most Common Negative Coping Strategies

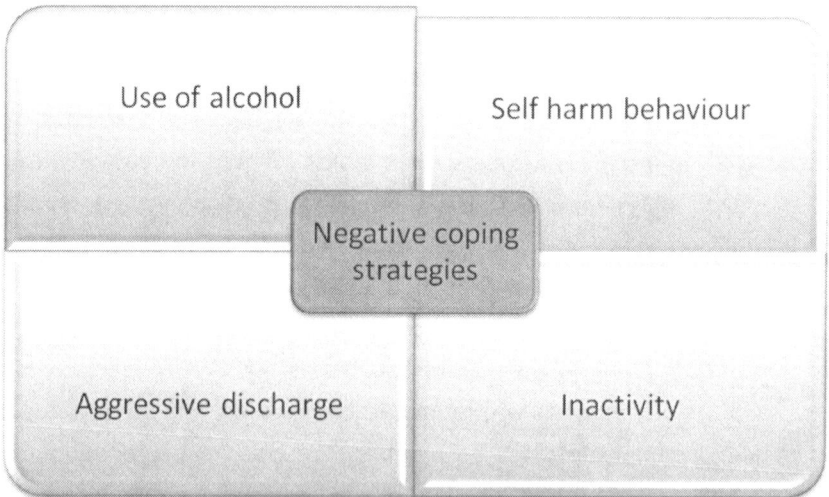

Use of alcohol

Self harm behaviour

Negative coping strategies

Aggressive discharge

Inactivity

- ***High alcohol intake*** – Alcohol is one of the most common negative coping strategies you can employ. Alcohol and other sedative drugs can temporarily numb your emotions and make you feel relaxed for a short period of time. However, high consumption of alcohol will eventually distort your judgment, and will lead to inappropriate decision-making. In addition, alcohol will eliminate any control you might have over your impulses, resulting in uncontrolled aggressive outbursts. Excessive and long-term use of alcohol has serious emotional and physical consequences such as emotional instability, liver damage, duodenal ulcers, impaired cognition, alcohol dementia, heart failure, and, in severe cases, premature death.

- *Self-harming behaviour* - Self-harming behaviour is another common negative coping strategy, which involves conduct which may result in physical harm to the person. Self-harming behaviour is highly maladaptive and includes wrist-cutting, suicide attempts or other impulsive acting-out activities, which are mostly immature, attention-seeking, and are usually ineffective in solving the problems.

- *Aggressive, uncontrolled discharge of negative emotions* is another negative coping strategy which involves inappropriate aggressive outbursts as a way of solving your problems. The most common outlet of such uncontrolled emotional discharges involves the destruction of furniture and other household items in order to release your negative tension.

- *Inactivity:* Inactivity is practically the cessation of any goal-directed activities. Inactivity is making a conscious decision not to respond to any stressful situation. Doing nothing is a wait-and-see approach which might be helpful only in a situation which is beyond your control. However, in most cases, doing nothing is a bad strategy which often has catastrophic results.

What are Your Divorce Coping Strategies?

The next exercise requires you to identify your principal coping strategies and measure their effectiveness.

Table 9.3   Your Divorce Coping Strategies

My usual coping strategy is:	Yes	No	I feel it improves my physical symptoms		I feel it helps me to function	
			Yes	No	Yes	No
I use alcohol excessively						
I hurt myself						
I easily become aggressive						
I usually wait & do nothing						
I look for information & logically assess the options						
I carefully consider the various options before I decide what to do						
I often talk to my family/friends						
I often ask friends/ family for help						
Overall effectiveness						

Coping skills become effective when you feel good and able to face life challenges. However, excessive reliance on negative coping skills will lead to poor physical and emotional reactions and reduced ability to face life stresses.

What can You do to Manage Your Stress?

You can control your divorce-related stress by using any of the following activities:
- Create a stress diary
- Reach out for help
- Take medication

1. Create a Stress Diary

A stress diary will empower you and help you to control stress.

Creating a stress diary is an effective tool to manage your stress. A stress diary requires you to record every daily event and rank these based on their perceived impact on your emotions, your psychological wellbeing and on your behaviour. In addition, you need to formulate an alternative, more productive response to each event and see how the alternative response reduces your stress.

The stress diary requires you to list all your daily divorce-related events and evaluate their severity based on their impact on your emotions, thoughts and on your behaviour. Thereafter, you need to re-evaluate each event, and to formulate an alternative, more positive interpretation of the event. Once you get into the habit of recording your daily events and think of a positive alternative interpretation, you will see how your stress diminishes. Your previous maladaptive appraisal of the situation will transform into a more adaptive and productive method, which will ultimately reduce your stress.

The Stress Diary: *Daily Event Recording Log*
Your daily event recording log provided in Table 9.4. requires you to record daily any situation you encounter and observe how it affected you,

as well as to formulate an alternative appraisal of the event and to devise a more productive line of action.

Table 9.4.   Your Step 1 Daily Event Recording Log

The Stressful situation	Your stress Severity score 0 = none 10 = severe	Your emotional reaction	Your alternative interpreta-tion and reaction	Your stress Severity score 0 = none 10 = severe
1.example: you received the court summons	10	Panic	You will give your ex the fight he deserves. Call your lawyer and set an immediate appointment	4
2				
3				
4				
5				

Some events may be beyond your control and there is little you can do to change these. In such instances, the only way to cope with events like this is to learn how to accept them without worrying too much, and to be able to move on. Fortunately, in most cases you will be able to influence the impact of your various life situations on your emotions, thoughts and on your behaviour. Each time you encounter a new situation you need to try to identify the best and most practical reaction to adopt in order to minimise your stress. Regular completion of the stress diary will allow you to control what is happening in your life, and will thus minimise your stress.

2.   Getting Help

Having a good support network and being able to mobilise it to your advantage will be highly effective in reducing your stress. Contrary to your initial inclination, getting help from others is not necessarily a sign of weakness or a failure. On the contrary, getting help is a sign of strength. Good friends and a strong social network are some of the best methods you can adopt to manage your stress. Reaching out for emotional and material support is a highly effective coping skill which you should deploy in times of need. Research has shown that being lonely and socially isolated can increase your anxiety, rejection and depression. The ability to talk openly to a close friend who can listen empathetically, and who is able to give you sound advice, company and support will be highly effective in reducing your stress levels. On the other hand, if you don't have a support network your ability to handle stress is significantly impaired. The good news is that it is never too late to make new friendships, or to reach out and renew broken ties. To build new social bridges is not an easy task, especially during divorce, when you would prefer to hide and to minimise social contacts. However, getting involved with others is beneficial to your mental health and requires motivation and strong determination. Getting support from others must be a priority for you, as the bigger your support network is, the easier it becomes to manage your life and the less stressed you will be.

In general, there are two types of help that you can look for:
- Social help
- Professional help

A   The Social Network

The most common available social network includes:
- Best friends
- Trusted family members
- Work associates
- Self-help groups
- Religious organisations

The Role of Having a Best Friend

Having a good and reliable friend is priceless. A good friend is someone who is able to be there for you whenever you need him/her. A good friend can listen to your problems and can give you sound advice. Having a good and reliable friend also means that you can get practical help when you need to pick up your children from school or perhaps obtain a loan when you are short of money. Sharing your problems with someone and having a shoulder to lean on can significantly reduce your stress. Sometimes divorcing couples share the same best friend. In such an event, the best friend faces a huge conflict created by the presence of mixed loyalties. It is very difficult to maintain a good friendship with a couple which is at war and has secrets from one another. It is extremely important that you are able to understand the dilemma that the mutual friend faces. Overall, the mutual friend must feel comfortable, neutral and be loyal to you.

A Trusted Family Member

Nothing is a thicker then blood. During the divorce, turning to a close family member is the most reliable and sensible approach. The advantages of having a trusted family member upon whom you can rely are innumerable, as long as his/her loyalty to you and your case is guaranteed. However, getting family backing should not place the family members in any harmful position, and should not isolate them from the rest of the family.

Work Associates

During the divorce, the work environment can be seen as a trouble-free zone. The neutral atmosphere of the workplace with regard to your personal ordeal places your work associates in a favourable position. In most cases, the work arena provides the opportunity to build relationships with people who are not emotionally involved with your divorce. Therefore, the advice you get from your work associates can be more neutral and practical. In addition, the relationship you build with your work associates can divert your thoughts and worries from your private problems. Contrary to your initial inclination to avoid your co-workers and to keep them out of your personal affairs, you will be pleasantly surprised to see how much support and help you get from your work associates.

Self-Help Group

Self-help groups are composed of people who share a common problem or a common interest. The individuals who make up these groups are voluntary participants who try to face similar issues together. Belonging to a cohesive self-help group can provide additional support. Going through a divorce can lead to strong feelings of shame and guilt which drive you away from any social interaction. Attending self-help groups provides a forum through which to assess the problems you face, which are surprisingly similar to those of all the other group participants. You will realise that you and other group members are in the same boat, have similar problems and are experiencing similar feelings. Sharing your personal problems with the other group members will provide the right medium for receiving advice and observing how others solved their similar problems. You will be exposed to a wealth of information which will help you to cope more effectively with your divorce. Participation in self-help groups will also strengthen your sense of belonging and eliminate your natural tendency for social isolation.

Religious Organisations

Religious organisations may appeal to those who have strong religious faith and wide religious convictions. The religious community provides a social environment which has a common shared belief that enhances the mutual sense of belonging. Most religious organisations will have trained divorce counsellors who can provide support and counselling. In addition, religion can provide some people with answers to many difficult questions and solace for sore hearts.

B   The Professional Network

The most common available professional network includes:
- Your GP
- Counsellors
- Self-help books
- Psychologists
- Psychiatrists

Your Family GP

Your family physician is usually situated at the top of the professional hierarchy, as the GP is the obvious starting contact point on the professional ladder. Most GPs can provide basic emotional support and advice. However, in some cases, your family GP might be also treating your ex-spouse. In the event of having a mutual GP, this might place him/her in a difficult position which often causes mixed loyalty. In such cases, it is better to exclude your GP from your support network.

Self-Help Books & Internet
Self-help books and the internet contain a huge amount of information. However, the information you can get from open sources is mostly provided in a passive form which might have a somewhat limited effect on your stress levels. Self-help books are a much more reliable source of information compared to the internet which often has a questionable reliability. Self-help books can provide you with practical information about a range of divorce-related problems and can advise you about the possible ways and means to handle your divorce.

Counselling
Counsellors are trained professionals who can help you to manage your divorce-related emotional and practical problems. As a rule of thumb, you should feel comfortable talking to the counsellor, and should be able to convey your problems freely. During the counselling session, the counsellor will help you to focus on the current specific problem and will explore with you the possible solutions. Unfortunately, almost anyone can call him/herself a counsellor after having attended a short course. It is highly important that you do a background check before choosing a counsellor. You need to ask the counsellor about his/her professional training, his/her qualifications and his/her previous experience in handling similar divorce-related problems. Self-help groups or the local mental health agency are the best place to get a list of qualified and registered counsellors.

Mental Health Services
Mental health services employ highly trained clinical psychologists, social workers and psychiatrists. These mental health professionals receive basic professional training on how to manage major psychiatric disorders. However, not all of the mental health professionals receive adequate training

in the management of divorce-related issues. As a result, it is important to check beforehand regarding the therapist's training and experience in handling divorce-related issues. The support available from the mental health services should be used, as long as it is reliable and effective.

In Table 9.5 you can list all the support network providers available to you in your area.

Table 9.5   Your Support Network Options

Social Network	Availability		Reliability	
	Yes	No	Yes	No
Friends: who				
1				
2				
3				
Family members: who				
1				
2				
3				
Work associates				
1				
2				
3				
Self help group: which				
1				
2				
3				
Religious organisations				
1				
2				
3				

In Table 9.6 you can list all the mental health providers available to you in your area.

Table 9.6   Your Professional Support Options

Professional Network	Availability		Reliability	
	Yes	No	Yes	No
Physicians				
1				
2				
Counselors				
1				
2				
Psychologist				
1				
2				
Psychiatrists				
1				
2				
Social workers				
1				
2				

Medication and other forms of therapy for stress will be explained further in the chapter dealing with anxiety management.

Key Points

- The best way to manage divorce-related stresses is to use a stress diary regularly, as well as to become involved with a self-help group and with the available professional networks.
- The stress diary is a powerful tool for identifying the causes of your divorce-related stresses and providing alternative options on how to manage them.

Dr Shlomo Brook

- The creation of a social support network provides additional help to combat isolation and stress.
- In the case of severe stress-related symptoms that cause functional impairment, it is advisable to contact your local mental health provider for further assessment and treatment.

Suggested reading

1. Talbott, S.M. (2002). *The Cortisol Connection.* Hunter House Inc.
2. Charlesworth, E.A and Nathan, R.G. (1984). *Stress management.* Ballantine books.
3. Brewer, S. (1999). *The Ultimate Stress Buster.* London: Ebury Press.
4. Powell, T. (2000). *Stress Free Living.* DK Publishing, inc.

TEN

Anxiety and Divorce

"Pessimism never won any battle".
D. Eisenhower

The Purpose

The purpose of this chapter is to explain the different aspects of divorce-related anxiety.

Introduction

Anxiety is a common, universal emotional reaction experienced by all mammals. Anxiety originates in specialised brain areas and results in mental and physical symptoms which are similar to fear of an unknown situation.

The mental and the physical symptoms of anxiety are disproportionate to any given situation, and interfere with an individual's daily functions. Epidemiological studies conducted in the US by Kessler revealed that 29% of all adults develop anxiety symptoms at some point in their lifetime. The management of anxiety disorders creates an enormous financial burden on the US economy. According to Greenberg, its annual cost amounts to $42 billion to the US tax payer. The most prevalent form of anxiety is known as generalised anxiety disorder which, according to Kessler, affects 5.1% of the US population.

Anxiety is extremely common during divorce due to the presence of severe stress, intense interpersonal and intra-personal conflicts and fear of the unknown future.

According to Wittchen, females tend to report anxiety symptoms more often than males, with a sex difference ratio of 2:1 which figure becomes higher in unmarried females.

It is speculated that the reason for such a sex difference resides in the fact that women generally tend to become more anxious when facing inter- and intra-personal conflicts, while men facing similar situations more often tend to externalise their emotional reactions and react with anger instead.

As mentioned earlier, all humans are intimately familiar with anxiety. Anxiety is widely experienced from an early age, and most probably, the first anxiety symptoms develop upon the separation from the safe environment of the mother's womb. However, the initial anxiety mostly remains unconscious. The early recollection of anxiety symptoms can be traced to childhood experiences associated with separation from caregivers. The first day in the nursery school is a common cause of anxiety for both a mother and her child. The anxiety develops as the result of the toddler's separation from his/her parent to be taken care of by an unfamiliar caregiver.

Severe childhood separation anxiety can indicate future similar reactions later in life, especially in any event of future separations. In addition, anxiety can develop whenever there is an unfamiliar or unknown situation. That's why it is very common to feel anxious before taking an exam, or before going on a first date, or before an interview for a new job.

Anxiety can be also associated with pleasurable activities such as going on holiday in an unfamiliar place.

Fortunately, in most cases, anxiety is transient and is short-lived, tending to fade away once the event is over. However, anxiety can be extremely prominent, and can last for long periods of time with a severe impact on the level of functioning. Pursuant to the length of the divorce processes and to the amount of conflicts these generate, anxiety can be experienced for a long period of time, and in some cases, may become chronic. Short-lived, mild anxiety is a natural response to stress, while chronic anxiety is an unnatural, pathological and incapacitating phenomenon. Having severe anxiety symptoms will negatively affect decision-making and functionality. Therefore, it is vital to treat anxiety as quickly as possible, in order to optimise daily functioning, and to be able to cope with the divorce-related challenges.

Anatomy of Anxiety

Anxiety is created by the same brain structures involved with stress:
- The *amygdala*
- The *hippocampus*
- The *thalamus*
- The *prefrontal cortex*

The Amygdala

The *amygdala* is an almond-shaped structure which is situated inside the temporal lobe below the cortex, and it forms an important part of the limbic system which is a complex brain structure involved with emotions. The *amygdala* plays an important role in generating anxiety, stress and

135

other emotional reactions.

Animal models showed that electric stimulation of the *amygdala* elicits fearful behaviour, while animals with damaged *amygdala* have impaired fear responses.

The *amygdala*'s connection with anxiety stems from its role as the executive branch responsible for activating the muscles, the sympathetic nervous system and the production of stress hormones.

The Thalamus

The *Thalamus* is also located in the limbic system and acts as the relay station that receives all the external information and redirects this to the relevant brain centres involved in the formation of anxiety. The inter-connectivity of the limbic system parts and their relative functions is illustrated in Figure 10.1.

Figure 10.1   The Visual Alarm Pathway

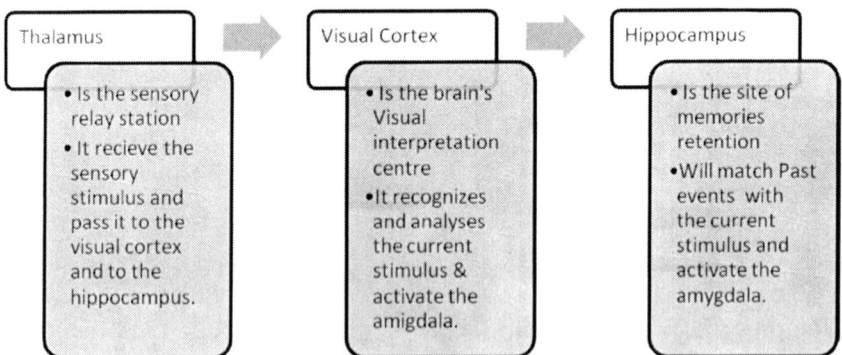

Thalamus	Visual Cortex	Hippocampus
• Is the sensory relay station • It recieve the sensory stimulus and pass it to the visual cortex and to the hippocampus.	• Is the brain's Visual interpretation centre •It recognizes and analyses the current stimulus & activate the amigdala.	• Is the site of memories retention •Will match Past events with the current stimulus and activate the amygdala.

The Prefrontal Cortex

The *prefrontal cortex* located in the anterior part of the brain is the area which processes the external stimulus and quantifies its dangerousness, evaluating the need for a reaction. The ultimate role of the *prefrontal cortex* is to give to the *amygdala* the on/off signal which is similar to the rider's control over his horse by means of the reins. Whenever the *prefrontal cortex* is under-active, the amygdale activity increases, resulting in anxiety.

The Hippocampus

The *hippocampus* is located in the temporal lobe as part of the limbic system.

The *hippocampus* stores memories of past fearful events and is responsible for matching them to new incoming information. A positive match eliminates the need to have unnecessary exposure to similar events which might be dangerous.

Studies have shown that anxious people tend to have a smaller *hippocampus* compared to healthy individuals. The activation of the limbic system centres results in anxiety which is illustrated in Figure 10.2.

Figure 10.2   The Anxiety Reaction

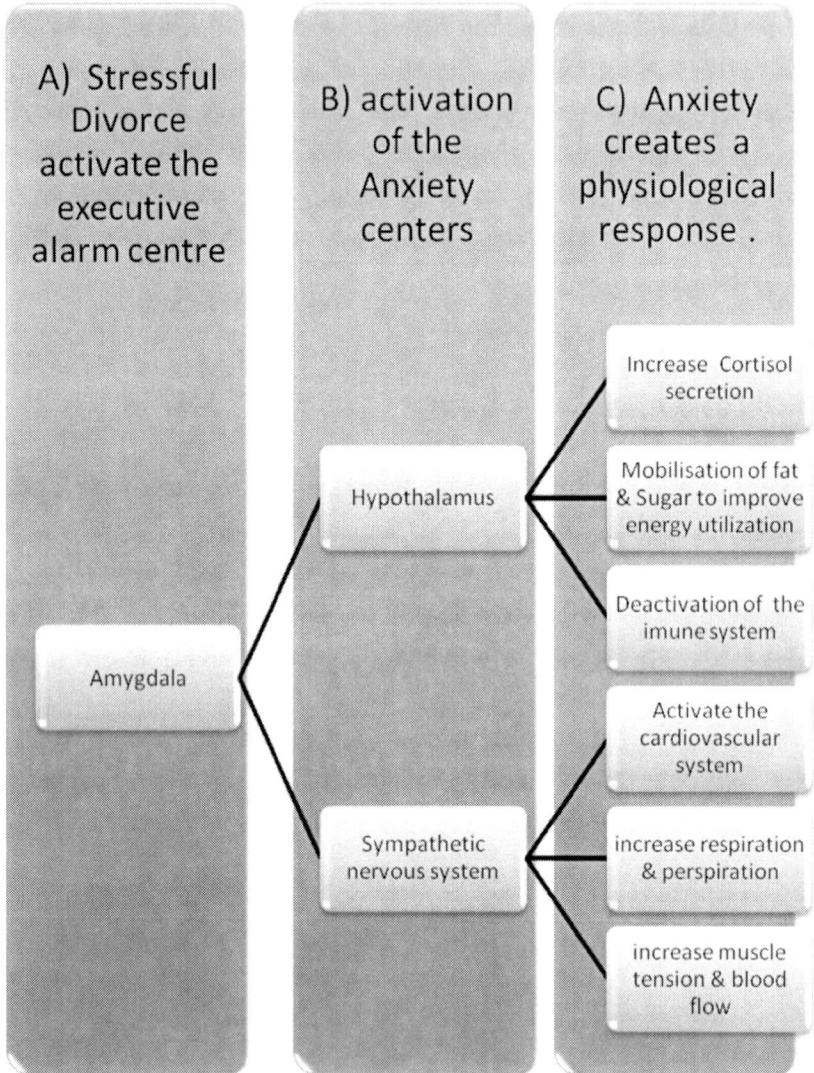

What are the Principal Neurotransmitters of Anxiety?

The brain is a complex and evolving organ. It consists of a myriad of interconnected brain cells called neurons. The neurons communicate with each other by chemicals called neurotransmitters. The neurotransmitters are released from the pre-synaptic neuron into the inter-neuronal space and activate their respective receptor which is situated on the post-synaptic neurons.

In other words, the neurotransmitters act like a coded language with which the neurons talk and share information.

The principal anxiety-related neurotransmitters are:

- GABA
- Serotonin
- Norepinephrine

GABA

The GABA is the brain's principal inhibitory neurotransmitter which is responsible for blocking excess neuronal activity. The GABA's highest concentration is in the substantia nigra, and in the hypothalamus. Low GABA levels may result in hyper-excitation of the brain's cells which could lead to uncontrolled seizure activities.

Serotonin (5-HT)

Serotonin is predominantly an activating neurotransmitter, and has the highest concentration in the raphe which is directly connected with the limbic system. Serotonin is involved with anxiety depression, as well as with sleep and appetite modulation.

Norepinephrine (NE)

The norepinephrine (NE) is a predominantly activating neurotransmitter which has the highest concentration in the *locus ceruleus* - a brain area also connected to the limbic system and involved with hyper-arousal, hyper-vigilance and hypertension states. In addition, the Norepinephrine is also involved with attention, mood, memory and pain sensation. Anxiety is the result of the intricate interplay between GABA, NE and the Serotonin.

The interplay between the principal anxiety-related neurotransmitters is illustrated in Figure 10.3.

Figure 10.3   The Anxiety Neurotransmitters and Their Functions

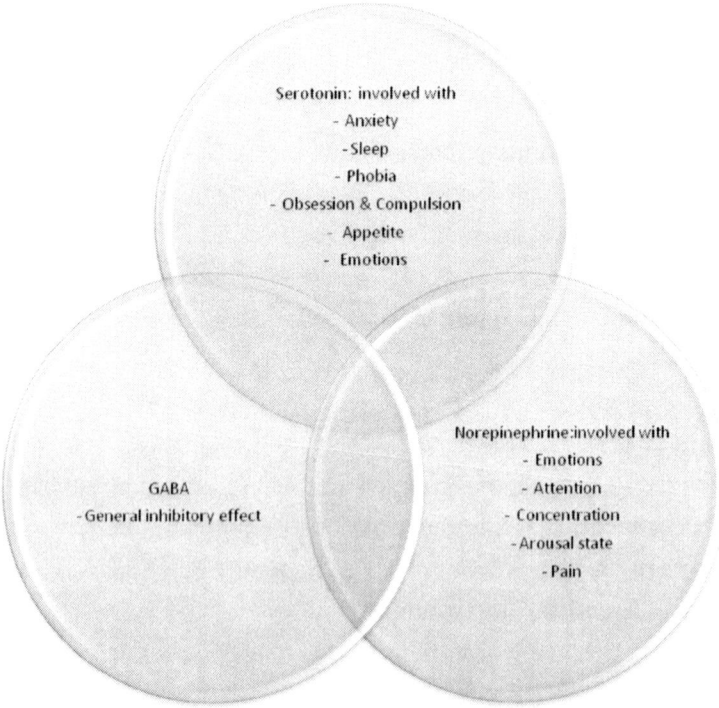

Serotonin: involved with
- Anxiety
- Sleep
- Phobia
- Obsession & Compulsion
- Appetite
- Emotions

GABA
- General inhibitory effect

Norepinephrine:involved with
- Emotions
- Attention
- Concentration
- Arousal state
- Pain

Symptoms of Anxiety

Anxiety manifests in a variety of physical, emotional, cognitive and behavioural symptoms which can severely impact on your daily functionality.

Anxiety can be experienced daily or intermittently, with multiple symptoms with various degrees of intensity as illustrated in Table 10. 4.

Table 10.4   Anxiety Symptoms

Physical component	Emotional component	Behavioral component	cognitive component
•muscle tension •fast heart beat •sweating •fast breathing •frequent urination •chest pain •diarrhoea •dry mouth •dizziness •hypertension •stomach butterflies •hot flashes •tingling sensation	•fearful •restlessness •hopeless •apprehensive expectation •feeling under pressure •feeling frustrated •easily tearful	•hyper alert •sleep problems •juminess •headache •easily fatigued •irritability •feeling dizzy •overactivity •tremor	•fearful •worry •reduced concentration •fear of losing control •fear of going crazy •fear of dying •feeling mentally drained •unable to make decisions •fear of social embarrassment

What are Your Anxiety Symptoms?

You can record your own anxiety symptoms in Table 10.5.

Table 10.5 What are Your Anxiety Symptoms?

Physical	Emotional	Behavioral	Cognitive
• _____	• _____	• _____	• _____
• _____	• _____	• _____	• _____
• _____	• _____	• _____	• _____
• _____	• _____	• _____	• _____
• _____	• _____	• _____	• _____
• _____	• _____	• _____	• _____
• _____	• _____	• _____	• _____

The Daily Anxiety Log

Anxiety symptoms can fluctuate daily with varying degrees of severity. Table 10.6 is a daily anxiety log in which you can record your anxiety symptoms and measure their intensity and their severity.

Mark with an X your anxiety symptoms daily and add up your daily score in the appropriate place. The exercise should preferably be carried out at night.

Table 10.6   The Daily Anxiety Log

Anxiety level		Anxious	Tense	Worried	Frightened
No symptoms	0				
Feel minimal symptoms	1				
Mild symptoms	2				
Moderate symptoms	3				
Panicking	4				
Daily Total score					

Anxiety level		Racing heart	Shaking	Can't breath	Chest pain
No symptoms	0				
Feel minimal symptoms	1				
Mild symptoms	2				
Moderate symptoms	3				
Panicking	4				
Daily Total score					

Anxiety level		Hot flushes	Choking	Nausea	Feeling dizzy
No symptoms	0				
Feel minimal symptoms	1				
Mild symptoms	2				
Moderate symptoms	3				
Panicking	4				
Daily Total score					

Dr Shlomo Brook

Anxiety level		Muscle tension	Frequent urination	Pins & needles	Dry mouth
No symptoms	0				
Feel minimal symptoms	1				
Mild symptoms	2				
Moderate symptoms	3				
Panicking	4				
Daily Total score					

Total daily anxiety score	Day 1	Day 2	Day 3	Day 4	Day 5	Day 6	Day 7

Interpretation of your daily score on the daily anxiety log:

0 - 16	*Normal anxiety range:* You experience minimal anxiety symptoms that have no impact on your day-to-day functions
17 - 32	*Mild anxiety:* You experience some symptoms which cause minimal distress
33 - 48	*Moderate anxiety:* Symptoms may cause some distress
49 - 64	*Severe anxiety:* Symptoms can lead to a high level of distress and can be incapacitating

Beside the physical and emotional part, anxiety also exhibits a cognitive component. The following section elaborates on the cognitive effects of anxiety.

Fear and divorce

Fear is a common innate emotional state imprinted in the human genome after millions of years' exposure to danger. Dangerous incidents become stored in the human genetic makeup, and promptly activate fearful thoughts and anxiety in the event of exposure to danger or to unknown situations.

Recognition of danger gets stored in the hippocampus which activates an immediate instinctual response to danger. An encounter with a snake is a perfect example of such an efficient instinctual reaction to a threat. You don't have to have been bitten by a snake in order to know that it

147

is dangerous. You instinctively recognise the potential danger of such an encounter.

Although divorce is not as bad as a snake bite, it is still highly stressful to most people. Your life and your future is unpredictable, and depends on other external factors such as your legal team and the courts. You have less control over your life as it is partially placed in the hands of other professionals. Therefore, fear becomes a natural reaction to divorce.

What are the Most Common Fears of Divorced People?

The most common fears of divorced people are listed as follows:
*   Fear of losing your children
*   Fear of being lonely
*   Fear of losing your property
*   Fear of becoming socially marginalised
*   Fear of being blamed for the divorce

All of the abovementioned fears are extremely common during the divorce and are often associated with the lack of control.

Self-doubt regarding your ability to form new relationships is frightening and is extremely prevalent at the early stages of divorce, as dating new people is highly stressful, especially if the last time it occurred was many years ago.

Having sex with a stranger other then your partner is also not an easy emotional exercise for most people. The blend of self-doubt and fear of the unknown become a lethal combination that can easily fuel fear and anxiety.

Other fears associated with divorce involve self-doubt regarding your ability to raise your children alone, or worries regarding your ability to handle your financial future. The fears of losing your house or becoming destitute are common concerns during the divorce.

Having a sense of control over life events is the best antidote for fear. You need to identify your most prominent fears and how anxious they can make you feel.

Table 10.7   The Daily Fear log

Fearful thought	Worse in the ...			Anxiety level 1 = minimal, 5 = maximal				
	Morning	Noon	Evening	1	2	3	4	5

Worry & Divorce

Worry is another cognitive component of anxiety. Worry involves thoughts or images which are capable of generating feelings of anxiety.

The worrying thoughts are analytical **ideations** which aim to resolve a specific problem. However, due to their inability to solve the specific problem, the thoughts or images tend to repeat endlessly, creating more uncertainty and anxiety.

Worrying also tends to magnify the problem and highlights only its possible negative outcome, resulting in anxiety.

Some people are more worry-orientated than others. The worriers tend to be perfectionists with a stronger need for control over their environment who are less tolerant of uncertainty. The inherent aim of the worry process is to gain some control over the situation, while failure to achieve such a goal results in anxiety.

The worry circle is illustrated in Figure 10.8.

Figure 10.8 The Worry Circle

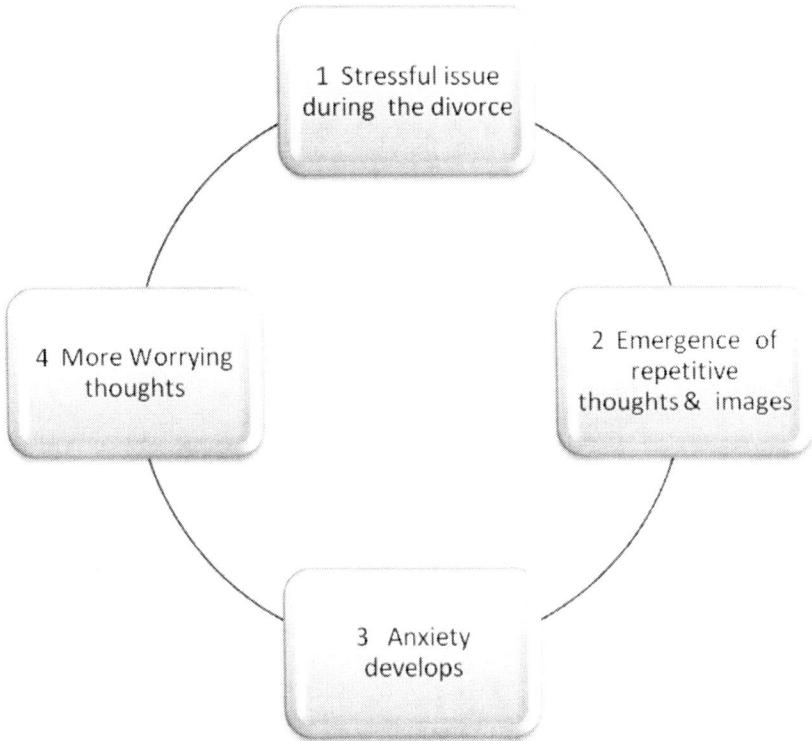

```
                    ┌──────────────────┐
                    │ 1 Stressful issue │
                    │ during the divorce│
                    └──────────────────┘

┌──────────────────┐                    ┌──────────────────┐
│ 4 More Worrying   │                    │ 2 Emergence of   │
│    thoughts       │                    │    repetitive    │
│                   │                    │ thoughts & images│
└──────────────────┘                    └──────────────────┘

                    ┌──────────────────┐
                    │   3 Anxiety       │
                    │   develops        │
                    └──────────────────┘
```

A divorce court hearing is a perfect example of how excessive worry can develop. Upon getting the court summons, you become preoccupied with endless thoughts and images about the court appearance. You continuously think and imagine the worst case scenario. You become anxious at the prospect of not getting what you want from the divorce. Eventually, your excessive preoccupation with the upcoming court case interferes with your work resulting in poor work performance.

Low self-esteem often accompanies worrying ideations resulting in clinging behaviour with a constant need for assistance and reassurance. In addition, worry is an active process which tends to expand from one specific divorce-related issue into many other life areas.

What can Trigger Your Worries?

Worry requires an initial cue that will trigger it. The initial cue that can trigger the worry process can be either internal or external:

- *An external trigger* is any external event that can generate fear and worry.
- *An internal trigger* is any mental image, thought or bodily sensation that can trigger your worry.

This is illustrated in Figure 10.9.

Figure 10.9 The Worry Triggers

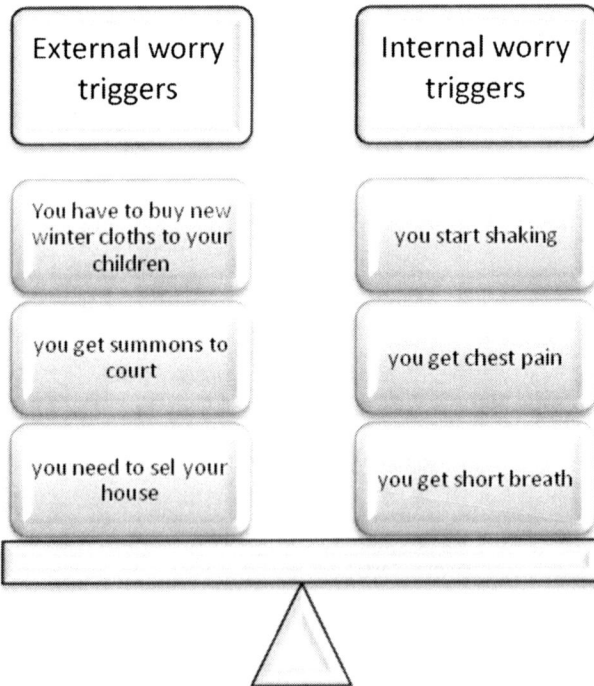

The ability to control your worries requires you to identify what can trigger them. Completion of Table 10.10, the worry trigger log will help you to identify the main events that can trigger your excessive worries.

10.10   The Worry Trigger Anxiety Logs

The external worry triggers	Worse in the ...			Anxiety level 1 = minimal, 5 = maximal				
	Morning	Noon	Evening	1	2	3	4	5
The internal worry triggers								

Once you are able to identify the causes of your worries and fears and their anxiety-provoking levels, you will be in a better position to control them. The next chapter will focus on the management of anxiety.

Key Points

- Divorce is one of the most common anxiety-provoking life events.
- Anxiety involves the activation of various brain structures situated in the *prefrontal cortex* and the limbic system.
- Anxiety involves the secretion of serotonin and norephinephrin.
- Anxiety causes multiple physical cognitive and behavioural symptoms.
- Fear and worry are the cognitive manifestations of anxiety.

References

1. Kessler, R.C., Berglund, P., Demler, O.(2005). Lifetime prevalence and age of onset distribution of DSM 4 disorders. *Arch Gen Psychiatry*, 62(6): 593-602.
2. Greenberg. P.E., Sisitsky, T., Kessler, R.C. (1999). The economic burden of anxiety disorders. *J. Clin Psychiatry*, 60 (7): 427-435.
3. Kessler, R.C., McGonagle, K.A. (1994). Lifetime prevalence of DSM 3 R psychiatric disorders in the US. *Arch Gen Psychiatry*, 51 (1): 8-19.
4. Wittchen, H.U., Zhao, S., Kessler, R.C. (1994). Generalized Anxiety in the National Comorbidity Survey. *Arch Gen Psychiatry*, 51 (5): 355-364.
5. Craske, G., Rapee, R., Jackel, L. & Barlow, D. (1989). Qualitative dimensions of worry. *Behaviour Research & Therapy*, 27: 397 – 402.

Suggested Reading

1. Wehrenberg, M & Prinz, S.M., M.D. (2007). *The anxious brain.* W.W. Norton & Company.
2. Nutt, D., Rickels, K & Stein, D. (2002). *Generalized Anxiety Disorder.* Martin Dunitz.
3. *Professional's handbook of psychotropic drugs.* (2001). Springhouse Corporation.
4. Arana, G.W & Rosenbaum, J.F. (2000). *Handbook of Psychiatric therapy.* Lippincott, W.W.
5. Rygh, J.L & Sanderson, W.C. (2004). *Treating Generalized Anxiety Disorder.* The Guilford press.
6. Leahy, R.L. (2003). *Cognitive therapy techniques a practitioner's guide.* The Guilford press.
7. Elkin, A. (1999). *Stress management for dummies.* Wiley Publishing, inc.
8. Westbrook, D., Kennerley, H & Kirk, J. (2008). *An introduction to Cognitive Behaviour Therapy.*Sage Publication.
9. Weiten, W. (1992). *Psychology themes & variations.* Wadsworth: Brooks/Cole Publishing Company.
10. *Encyclopaedia of Mental Health.* (1998). Academic Press.
11. Tallis (1994). The phenomenology of non-pathological worry: A preliminary investigation. In G. Davey & F. Tallis (eds). *Worrying: perspective on theory, assessment and treatment* (61-89) Chicester, England: John Willey.

ELEVEN

Divorce Anxiety Management

"A man can't ride your back unless it's bent"
Rev. Martin Luther King Jr.

The Purpose

The purpose of this chapter is to explain the different treatment modalities for your divorce-related anxiety.

Worry & Divorce: How You can Solve Them?

During the divorce process, and sometimes long after your divorce has been finalised, you may experience excessive worries over multiple issues which require your immediate attention. Often, even fewer serious issues can be magnified and over-exaggerated.

A study conducted by Craske found that people who suffer from generalised anxiety reported worrying 60.7% of the day compared to the average healthy individuals who spent only 18.2% of their day worrying.

The presence of excessive anxiety and worry can interfere with your ability to handle regular daily requirements as well as your ability to handle the divorce. Anxiety is not just a temporary and unpleasant experience. It can deteriorate and can precipitate a depressive state, as well as preventing you from reaching your potential and achieving your goals. Therefore anxiety should be treated as quickly as possible in order to improve your functionality and your ability to handle the divorce needs.

The following 5 step 'Worry Buster' will help you to reduce your excessive anxiety and worries.

The 5 Step Worry Buster

Step One: Find out the Format of your Worry Mechanism

The first step towards managing your worries requires you to establish whether you are a visual or a cognitive worry type.

- *The Visual Type*:
  In the visual worry form, your worry takes the form of an image. The visual worry form is a mental attempt to face a problematic situation by creating a mental image of the situation along with several ways to handle it.
  An example of visual worry is when you imagine a forthcoming event which you are unable to handle properly. The imagined situation and your shortcomings make you feel anxious and inadequate.

- *The Cognitive Type:*
  In the cognitive form, your worry takes the form of a repetitive thought.
  The thought has an unpleasant flavour and usually highlights your inadequacy.
  An example of a cognitive worry is when you have a frightening

and repetitive thought about a future situation which you manage poorly.

Your Worry is Primarily:

A) Visual ☐

B) Cognitive ☐

Step Two: Establishing What Makes You Feel Anxious and Causes You to Worry

The second step of the Worry Buster requires you to identify what makes you worry and how concerned you feel about it. In other words, do you really believe in what you think or imagine? Take some time to reflect about your divorce-related issues and your other daily problems and complete the following Table, 11.1. Remember the value percentages you assign to each worry are subjective therefore, even a tiny problem can still be a major issue for you.

Table 11.1   Identifying What Makes You Worry

What makes you worry?	How concerned you are about it?			To what extent do you believe it will happen?		
	Mild <30%	Moderate 30%-60%	Severe 61%-100%	Little	Somewhat	A lot
Example: I will be financially broke after divorce			X			X
Example : I will not be able to support myself			X			X
Example: I am never going to have a new relationship		X		X		
Example: I will lose my children			X		X	

Worries, like debts, tend to grow if they are not promptly resolved. In addition, unresolved issues tend to spill over to other issues eventually making you worry about almost anything on earth. Once you manage to identify the issues that make you anxious, you need to monitor their anxiety potential daily.

Step Three: Monitor Your Worries – The Worry Diary

The worry diary is an effective tool to measure the anxiety levels created by your worrying thoughts and images. For this exercise, you need to complete the following Table, 11.2's daily worry diary. Remember that the issues that make you worry are personal and subjective.

Table 11.2   The Daily Worry Diary

Date & Time	What makes you to worry	What are the thoughts & images that make you worry?	Anxiety level 0 = none 5 = moderate 10 = extreme
1			
2			
3			
4			
5			
6			
7			
8			
9			

A daily assessment of the issues that make you anxious and cause you to worry will increase your awareness and insight into the anxiety-provoking situations, which will be the first step towards recovery.

Step Four: The Positive Image Replacement

This step is an important element in the management of excessive worries as it will teach you how to change a dysfunctional anxiety-provoking image or thought into a more pleasant and functional one.

Worries appear in the form of a repetitive dysfunctional thought or image which has an obsessive quality. The anxiety-provoking thought or image quickly dominates your entire mental awareness and resists any attempt you make to get rid of it.

The human brain is programmed to focus on only one issue at any given moment, thus you are able to concentrate on only one thought at a time. Your thoughts replace one another at a rapid rate, lasting only for a brief period. There is no means to contemplate two or more thoughts at any given moment. The clinical implication of this inability to process two different thoughts at any given moment means that, if you can actively replace the dysfunctional image with a positive thought or a positive image, you will be able to reduce your anxiety levels.

The anxiety buster ability of a positive image replacement is illustrated in Figure 11.3.

Illustration 11.3: Positive Image Replacement Process

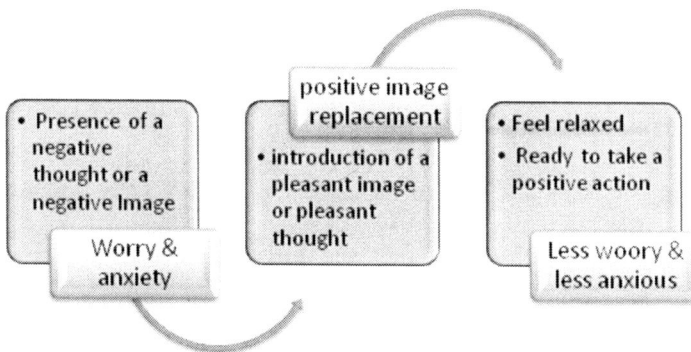

In the positive thought or image replacement exercise you need to replace each negative thought or image with a positive one. The presence of the positive thought or image will block any dysfunctional negative worrying alternative thought from accessing your mental awareness, and will subsequently reduce your anxiety. Practice *the positive thought/image replacement regularly* and you will master your anxiety. *Remember, what you visualise in your mind will affect your physical experience!*

The first step requires you to make a list of issues and situations that make you worry, based on their severity potential. Start your list with the least anxiety-provoking image or thought, and move up to the most anxiety-provoking situation. At the same time you need to consider a positive, relaxing alternative image. Once your list is complete, you can move on to the second step which is the actual practice.

Start with the least worrying thought or image and focus on your positive alternative. Initially, you will have to force yourself to think or hold the positive image, as your mind will automatically drift back to the negative dysfunctional thought. Try to hold the positive thought or image for as long as you can, and monitor any change in your anxiety levels and record the changes in Table 11.4. You need to keep repeating the same exercise until you are able to reduce your anxiety to reasonably low levels. Once you are able to master minor issues, you can proceed to the more anxiety-provoking issues until you can master your anxiety. Move along your worry list slowly and only once you are able to reduce your anxiety significantly.

Remember, you don't have to complete this exercise in one shot. Take your time; feel comfortable with the exercise, until you are able to master the thought replacement process effectively. Feel free to stop at any time and re-rank the original negative worrying thoughts as well as the alternative positive replacements with more effective ones, if you feel that your original replacement image did not achieve the goal you set.

Table 11.4   Positive Thought / Image Replacement Practice:

The worry thought / image	Your positive alternative	Anxiety level changes 0% ⇩ 100% less
1		
2		
3		
4		
5		

Practice the thought / image replacement exercise as often as you can. You can do it in your car while you are waiting for your children outside the school, or in your bed, as long as it is effective in reducing your anxiety.

Step Five: Use Positive Self-Talk

Self-talk is a cognitive exercise in which you encourage yourself by complementing your actions with positive feedback on your actions. Examples of positive self-talk remarks are: "I can do this", or "I am good", or "I did it".

Self-talk is practised regularly outside your mental awareness. Self-talk operates in the background, constantly ruminating on your behaviour. Your reactions to the day-to-day requirements are regularly monitored by yourself, providing constant feedback on your performance. During the divorce process, pursuant to your reduction in self-esteem, your reactions to life circumstances tend to produce negative, self-degrading comments which further reduce self-esteem and increase the potential for anxiety. Higher awareness of positive self-talk and the advantages of replacing negative comments with positive ones can significantly reduce your anxiety levels and improve your self-esteem.

Due to the automatic qualities of self-talk, you are normally unaware of its existence, and you never challenge its content. The results of having continuous negative self-talk are anxiety and low self-esteem. On the other hand, cultivating regular positive, encouraging, and motivating realistic self-talk can increase your self-esteem and eliminate anxiety.

Illustration 11.5 illustrates the emotional and psychological effects of positive and negative self-talk.

Illustration 11.5   **Emotional and Psychological Effects of Self-Talk**

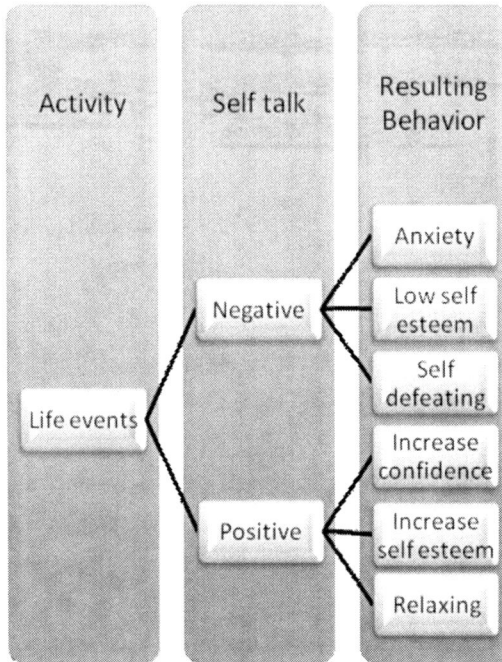

During the divorce, negative self-talk is highly prominent due to the presence of low self-esteem, self-doubt about making the right decisions, and worries about the unknown future.

You may often hear yourself saying:

- " I'm trapped"
- " I'm never going to cope with this situation"
- "What if I never find a job?"
- "I can't go through this"
- " I'm a loser"

These negative "voices" are automatic comments you make regarding your life situation. Engaging in constant negative self-talk will increase your anxiety and will prevent you from taking active, positive steps in order to successfully manage the challenges ahead. However, if you can regularly use positive self-talk, you will be able to face your daily needs more efficiently and with minimal stress and anxiety.

Examples of positive self-talk are:

- "I did well"
- "I'm good"
- "I can do this"
- "I handled the situation rather well"

Change Your Negative Self-Talk into Positive

The first step in fighting negative self-talk is to become aware of its existence. Commonly, during the divorce, your self-talk is negative and unchallenged. Analysis of your self-talk style will reveal its negative and degrading nature.

However, the good news is that you can learn how to replace your automatic negative self-talk with self-talk of a more positive nature. In the following exercise you need to identify your negative self-talk style and the amount of anxiety this causes, replacing it with positive self-comments and measuring their relaxing impact.

Table 11.6   The Self-Talk Modifier

Your negative Self talk "voice"	Anxiety level: 0 = no anxiety . . . . 10 = Extremely anxious	Positive self talk replace-ment	Anxiety level: 0 = no anxiety . . . . 10 = Extremely anxious
1.			
2.			
3.			
4.			
5.			

Try to use positive self-talk regularly and see how it reduces your anxiety and improves your confidence.

2)   **Engage in Pleasurable Activity**

During your divorce there is often little time available to engage in pleasurable activities. Coping with your daily needs requires major adjustment and lots of sacrifices. You automatically tend to focus on the most important activities such as keeping your daily routine going, coping with your work demands and your household chores, while overlooking the "less important" pleasurable activities.

In addition, having high anxiety levels, you tend to limit your social involvement due to your reduced self-esteem and self-confidence. You feel guilty of "wasting time" doing something that might be seen as less important.

The net result of such a negative attitude is limited involvement in any relaxing activity that might potentially make you feel good. On the other hand, if you immerse yourself in a balanced lifestyle which requires you to be involved in relaxing activities then your anxiety levels will substantially reduce.

The first step towards obtaining such a goal is to identify those activities that can potentially make you feel good, and then incorporate the most rewarding activities into your daily schedule.

Table 11.7   The Pleasure Activities Log

Day & Time	Scheduled Activity	Level of pleasure		Anxiety level changes:
		Predicted Potential pleasure: 0 = no pleasure	Actual pleasure 0 = no pleasure	0%
		10 = highly pleasurable	10 = highly pleasurable	100% Reduction
Monday 17:00	*Example: Going to gym*	*6*	*8*	*80%*

3)   **Muscle Relaxation**

Muscle relaxation is a simple technique which you can use to reduce your anxiety. Muscle relaxation is a physical exercise which requires you to contract your major muscle groups, one at a time for 10 seconds and then relax them. You can use the muscle relaxation technique as much as you want without fear of causing damage. You should preferably allocate a quiet room without any external interference for this purpose, and use a comfortable chair.

Sit on the chair, close your eyes and clear your mind of disturbing thoughts.

Start with your lower muscle group and move slowly upwards.

- Point your toes outward and tense them for 10 seconds, then relax and pause for 5 seconds. Repeat the exercise and move on to your next muscle group.
- Tense your lower leg muscles for 10 seconds then relax and pause for 5 seconds. Repeat the exercise and move on to the next muscle group.
- Tense your thigh muscles for 10 seconds then relax and pause for 5 seconds. Repeat the exercise and move on to the next muscle group.
- Tense your hip muscles for 10 seconds then relax and pause for 5 seconds. Repeat the exercise and move on to the next muscle group.
- Tense your abdominal muscles for 10 seconds then relax and pause for 5 seconds. Repeat the exercise and move on to the next muscle group.
- Tense your chest muscles for 10 seconds then relax and pause for 5 seconds. Repeat the exercise and move on to the next muscle group.
- Tense your back muscles for 10 seconds then relax and pause for

5 seconds. Repeat the exercise and move on to the next muscle group.

- Tense your lower arm muscles for 10 seconds then relax and pause for 5 seconds. Repeat the exercise and move on to the next muscle group.
- Tense your upper arm muscles for 10 seconds then relax and pause for 5 seconds. Repeat the exercise and move on to the next muscle group.
- Tense your shoulder area muscles for 10 seconds then relax and pause for 5 seconds. Repeat the exercise and move on to the next muscle group.
- Tense your jaw muscles for 10 seconds then relax and pause for 5 seconds. Repeat the exercise and move on to the next muscle group.
- Tense your mouth muscles for 10 seconds then relax and pause for 5 seconds. Repeat the exercise and move to the next muscle group.
- Tense your eye muscles by closing your eyes tightly for 10 seconds then relax and pause for 5 seconds. Repeat the exercise and move on to the next muscle group.
- Tense your forehead for 10 seconds then relax and pause for 5 seconds. Repeat the exercise one more time. Once you have finished, stay relaxed on your seat for several minutes.

During the exercise take a deep breath slowly through your nose and exhale slowly.

You will notice that within several minutes of doing muscle relaxation exercises you feel calm and relaxed.

4)   **Medication**

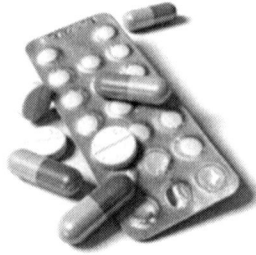

Anxiety symptoms can be highly distressing however they can be rapidly reduced through regular use of anxiolytic medications.

Benzodiazepines (BNZ) are the most common medication used for the treatment of anxiety symptoms. The BNZ has central nervous system depressant properties with a strong anti-anxiety effect at a lower dosage and sedative-hypnotic properties when used in higher doses.

The BNZ's extensive popularity stems from its effective anxiolytic effects as well as from its relative safety.

The first synthesized BNZ, Librium, was developed during the 1960s, and since then, more than 30 products have been developed and sold globally. From a chemical perspective, all BNZ share a common benzene ring fused with a diazepine ring.

All BNZ enhance the activity of GABA - the principal brain's inhibitory neurotransmitter.

What is GABA and How Does it Work?

GABA is a protein produced by specialised brain nerve cells from glutamate which inhibits the brain's nerve cell conduction. GABA is stored inside the cell, and upon its release it activates its corresponding GABA receptors located on the post-synaptic cell membranes.

The inhibitory effects of GABA on the cell conduction results from the opening of the chloride channels located inside the GABA receptors allowing the influx of Chloride ions into the nerve cell. The presence of a high concentration of intracellular chloride ions leads to hyperpolarisation of the cell membrane thus making it unresponsive to electrical transmission.

The structure of the GABA receptor is illustrated in Figure 11. 8.

Figure 11.8   The GABA Receptor

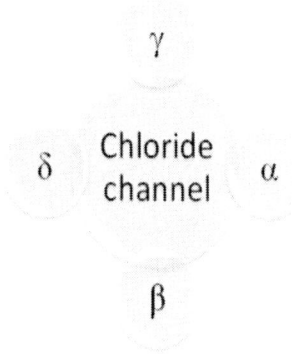

γ

δ Chloride channel α

β

What are the Clinical Effects of BNZs?

The most common clinical effects of BNZs are:
• Anxiolytic,
• Sedative
• Hypnotic
• Muscle relaxant
• Anti-convulsant

Due to these specific activities, BNZs are most commonly used in:
• Anxiety disorders
• Sleep disorders

- Seizures (Epilepsy)
- Muscle disorders

The BNZs' ability to relieve anxiety is due to their fast absorption rate and their high lipid solubility which enables them to penetrate the brain quickly. However, the biggest disadvantage of BNZ use is their tendency to cause dependency and withdrawal symptoms if discontinued abruptly.

Frequent use of BNZs can lead to tolerance of their anti-anxiety effects meaning that higher doses become needed to achieve the desirable effect. The tolerance to the anti-anxiety effect of BNZs is less than the tolerance to their hypnotic effect, resulting in the product's reduced ability to induce sleep after prolonged use, while maintaining their ability to reduce anxiety symptoms.

The sedative hypnotic properties of BNZs manifest by the decreased latency time in falling asleep, as well as by the prolongation of stage two of the non REM sleep waves. In other words, BNZs will make you sleep faster and stay sleeping longer.

The following section summarises the most common anti-anxiety medication:

Overview of the most common used BNZ and anti-anxiety medications

The Benzodiazepines: (BNZ)

Table 11.9   Alprazolam

How supplied	Tab. 0.25mg Tab. 0.5 mg Tab. 1 mg	Daily dose	Start 0.25 three times a day, increase, if needed, to a max. of 6 mg/day

Action	1. Enhancing the GABA inhibitory effect in the GABA receptors located at the limbic & subcortical areas.	Precautions	1. Urine retention 2. Impaired kidney, liver, lung 3. Glaucoma 4. Potential abuse & dependence 5. Avoid use if breastfeeding 6. Hypersensitivity to the product
Indication	1. Panic disorder. 2. Generalised anxiety 3. Insomnia	Contraindication	1 Acute angle glaucoma. 2. Hypersensitivity to the drug 3. Concomitant use of alcohol can enhance CNS depressant effect 4. Concomitant use of Kava Kava may cause coma
Absorption	1. Rapidly absorbed in the GI tract. Acts within 15 – 30 min. 2. Plasma peak level 1.5 H.	Metabolism	1. Liver: Has active & inactive metabolites
Excretion	Urine	Half-life	15 h.

Tips for use	1. Can be taken without regard of meals 2. Can be taken morning or evening 3. Avoid concomitant use of alcohol 4. Take precautions when driving or using heavy machines 5. Warning about potential abuse & dependence		
Side-Effect	Frequency		Special
	Common	Rare	consideration
Constipation	√		1. Use with caution
Flatulence		X	if you have sleep
Diarrhea		X	apnea or COPD
Nausea	√		(Chronic obstructive
Dry mouth	√		lung disease).
Dizziness	√		
Tachycardia		X	
Hypotension	√		
Confusion		X	
Drowsiness	√		
Weight gain		X	
Light-headedness	X		
Blurred vision	X		
Nasal congestion		X	
Syncope		X	

Table11.10   Diazepam

How supplied	Tab. 2mg, Tab. 5 mg Tab. 10 mg Oral solution 5mg/5ml	Daily dose	Start 2 – 10 mg twice daily, increase if needed to a max. of 60 mg/day
Action	1. Enhancing the GABA inhibitory effect in the GABA receptors at the limbic & subcortical areas.	Precautions:	1. Urine retention 2. Impaired kidney, liver, lung 3. Glaucoma 4. Potential abuse & dependence 5. Avoid use if breastfeeding 6. Hypersensitivity to the drug 7 Cautious use by the elderly
Indication	1. Panic disorder 2. Generalised anxiety 3. Insomnia	Contraindication	1 Acute angle glaucoma. 2. Hypersensitivity to the drug 3. Concomitant use of alcohol can enhance CNS depressant effect 4. Concomitant use of Kava Kava may cause coma

Absorption	1. Rapidly absorbed by the GI tract. Acts within 30 – 60 min. 2. Plasma peak level 1.5 H.	Metabolism	1. Liver. Has active metabolite desmethyldiazepam.
Excretion	Urine	Half-life	20 - 100 h.
Tips for use	1. Can be used without regard of meals 2. Can be taken morning or evening 3. Avoid alcohol as this enhances the potency of the medication 4. Take precautions when driving or using heavy machines 5. Warning about potential abuse & dependence		
Side-Effect	Frequency		Special consideration
	Common Rare		

Constipa-tion	√		1. Use with caution if you have sleep apnea or COPD (Chronic obstructive lung disease).
Nausea		X	
Urine retention		X	
Nausea	√		
Halluci-nations		X	
Dizziness	√		
Fatigue		X	
Hypoten-sion	√		
Confu-sion		X	
Drowsi-ness	√		
Jaundice		X	
Head-ache	X		
Skin rash		X	
Blurred vision		X	
Syncope		X	
Diplopia		X	
Nistag-mus		X	

Dr Shlomo Brook

Table 11.11   Lorazepam

How supplied	Tab. 0.25mg Tab. 1 mg Tab. 2 mg	Daily dose	Start 0.25 mg three times a day, increase if needed to a max. of 4 mg/day
Action	1. Enhancing the GABA inhibitory effect in the GABA receptors at the limbic & subcortical areas.	Precautions	1. Impaired kidney, liver, lung 2. Acute Angle Glaucoma 3. Potential abuse & dependence 4. Pregnancy particularly in 3rd trimester 5. Hypersensitivity to the product 6. Cautious use by the elderly and debilitated
Indication	1. Panic disorder 2. Generalised anxiety 3. Insomnia 4. Convulsion	Contraindication	1 Acute angle glaucoma 2. Hypersensitivity to the drug 3. Concomitant use of alcohol can enhance CNS depressant effect 4. Concomitant use of scopolamine may cause hallucination & irrational behaviour 5. Avoid use if breastfeeding 6. Safety of use by those under age 18 under study

Absorption	1. Rapidly absorbed in the GI tract. Acts within 15 – 30 min. 2. Plasma peak 2 H.	Metabolism	1. Liver. Has inactive metabolites
Excretion	Urine	Half-life	10 - 20 h.
Tips for use	1. Can be used regardless of meals 2. Can be taken morning or evening 3. Avoid concomitant use of alcohol 4. Take precautions when driving or using heavy machines 5. Warning about potential abuse & dependence		
Side Effect	Frequency Common Rare		Special consideration

Side effect			Notes
Constipation	√		1. Lorazepam is the preferred BNZ in patients with liver disease.
Flatulence		X	2. Use with caution if you have sleep apnea or COPD (Chronic obstructive lung disease).
Diarrhoea		X	
Nausea	√		
Dry mouth	√		
Dizziness	√		3. Use the largest dose at bedtime.
Tachycardia		X	
Hypotension	√		4. Intramuscular injection can cause amnesia (memory shut down).
Confusion		X	5. Discontinue gradually over a period of 8 – 12 weeks.
Drowsiness	√		
Light-headedness	X		
Blurred vision	X		
Amnesia	X		
Agitation		X	
Disorientation		X	

B)   Azapirones: (Not chemically related to BNZ)

Table 11.12   Buspirone

How supplied	Tab. 5mg Tab. 10 mg	Daily dose	Start 5mg three times a day, increase if needed every 3 days to a max. of 60 mg/ day
Action	1. Decreases serotonin activity & has pre-synaptic dopamine antagonist action. Onset of action between 7 days to a max. effect in 4 weeks	Precautions	1. Impaired kidney, liver 2. Hypersensitivity to the drug 3. Potential abuse & dependence 4. Avoid use if breastfeeding

Indication	1. Generalised anxiety.	Contraindi-cation	1 Concomitant use of MAOI which can cause hypertension 2. Hypersensitivity to the drug 3. Concomitant use of alcohol can enhance CNS depressant effect 4. Concomitant use of Digoxin which can lead to digoxin intoxication 5. Avoid concomitant use of Kava Kava which can cause sedation
Absorption	1. Rapidly absorbed in the GI tract. Presence of food slows absorption. 2. Plasma peak 1.5 H.	Metabolism	1. Liver. Has active metabolite 1-PP
Excretion	Urine 40% faeces	Half-life	2 - 11 h.

Tips for use	1. Should be used with meals 2. Can be taken morning or evening 3. Avoid concomitant use of alcohol 4. You must be prepared for its slowed & delayed onset of action		
Side-Effect	Frequency		Special consideration
	Common	Rare	
Abdominal distress	√		1. Less effective in patients who were treated previously with BNZs 2. Expect delayed on-set of action of at least 7 days.
Dry mouth		X	
Diarrhoea		X	
Nausea	√		
Blurred vision		X	
Dizziness	√		
Numbness		X	
Nervousness		X	
Light-headedness		X	
Drowsiness	√		

Clinical doses of BNZs can reduce worry symptoms by reducing the hypersensitivity to interpersonal circumstances thus improving anxiety. However, the psychological manifestation of anxiety is better managed with psychological and behavioural treatment modalities.

BNZs can either be used intermittently or continuously, based on the level and the anxiety frequency. The presence of high and continuous anxiety symptoms warrants the regular use of BNZs, while the irregular presence of anxiety requires only intermittent administration of BNZs.

The BNZs are especially effective in the state of hyper-arousal caused by autonomic hyperactivity.

The current pharmacological management of anxiety disorders is summarised in Table 11.13.

Table 11.13   Pharmacological Management of Anxiety Disorders

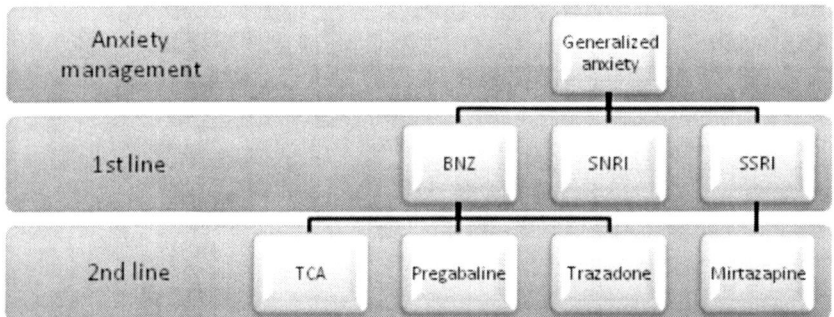

Anxiety management			Generalized anxiety	
1st line		BNZ	SNRI	SSRI
2nd line	TCA	Pregabaline	Trazadone	Mirtazapine

SNRI is a group of antidepressants which have a similar reuptake inhibitory activity on the Serotonin and Noradrenaline.

SSRI is a group of antidepressants which have a similar reuptake inhibitory activity on the Serotonin.

TCA is a group of old antidepressants which have a similar reuptake inhibitory activity on the Serotonin and Noradrenaline.

Mirtazapine and **Trazadone** are antidepressants with a more complex mode of action.

Pregabaline is a relatively new product derived from an old antiepileptic.

The use of antidepressant medications in the management of anxiety disorders will be thoroughly discussed in the depression section of the book.

The major clinical drawback of BNZs' use lies in their inherent tendency to cause dependence and withdrawal symptoms. Unfortunately, the daily use of the term 'dependence' is largely confused with that of addiction, thus often people using BNZs are seen as addicted. Such terminological confusion between addiction and dependence merits further discussion.

Addiction

Addiction is defined as a compulsive craving for a drug. Such craving develops pursuant to repeated administration of that specific drug. Addiction is always associated with a tolerance to the effect of the drug which requires a constant dose increase in order to achieve the required effect.

Addiction to any given drug leads to multiple cognitive, behavioural, emotional and physiological symptoms. In addition, *addiction leads to a compulsive use of the drug, as well as the inability to control its consumption despite its negative effects and the maladaptive consequences on the individual.*

Addiction usually causes severe medical problems, dysfunctional interpersonal relationships, failure to fulfil one's potential, as well as legal and economic complications. ***Addiction is not a common feature of BNZ use, and it is unlikely that sensible use of BNZs will lead to addictive behaviour.***

Having said that, it is common to find excessive use of BNZs among drug addicts, a fact which has probably contributed to the negative image of BNZs, thus, as a rule, BNZs should be avoided in those individuals with a history of addiction.

Dependence

Dependence on any drug is defined as the presence of pathological withdrawal symptoms upon the discontinuation of the drug. Withdrawal symptoms are also common after discontinuation of most psychotropic medications, including antidepressants. Upon abrupt discontinuation of BNZs, withdrawal symptoms often develop similar to those symptoms which occur after abrupt discontinuation of most antidepressant medications.

The dependence caused by BNZ use manifests as rebound anxiety symptoms upon abrupt discontinuation of the BNZs, as well as nervousness, anxiety, tremor, and loss of appetite. These withdrawal symptoms are slower to develop after using BNZ products with longer half-life such as diazepam, compared to those BNZs with a short half-life such as alprazolam.

In general, the physical and psychological withdrawal symptoms following BNZ discontinuation are far less prominent than the withdrawal symptoms which develop after antidepressant use, especially if the BNZs were used for a short period and at lower doses.

Unfortunately, the confusion and misunderstanding regarding the dependence and addiction terminology lead to social stigma, and a feeling of shame in those using BNZs, which has resulted in the failure to use BNZs properly for the treatment of anxiety disorders leading to inappropriate dosage and treatment failure. Such irregular and inappropriately low doses of BNZs result in continuous disabling anxiety symptoms and unnecessary ongoing suffering.

In general, the use of BNZ should be carefully and closely monitored by the therapist, as well as by patients and supporting family members. Psycho-education regarding the proper use of BNZ and the potential to develop withdrawal symptoms upon sudden discontinuation of BNZ is highly important for the successful treatment of anxiety symptoms.

BNZs should always be used in conjunction with the other psychological treatment modalities in order to maximise their anxiolytic effects and to minimise their total daily dose, as well as the duration of use. Long-term use of BNZs should be reserved for those individuals who are treatment resistant.

Key Points

- The regular use of the worry diary can reduce anxiety symptoms significantly.
- The regular practice of the thought / image replacement procedure can alleviate anxiety symptoms effectively.
- There are several pharmacological treatment modalities for anxiety disorder that include BNZs and antidepressant medications.
- BNZs are highly effective in reducing anxiety symptoms.
- Excessive BNZ use can lead to tolerance and dependence.

References

1. Kessler, R.C., Berglund, P., Demler, O. (2005). Lifetime prevalence and age of onset distribution of DSM 4 disorders. *Arch Gen Psychiatry*, 62(6):593-602.
2. Greenberg, P.E., Sisitsky, T., Kessler, R.C. (1999). The economic burden of anxiety disorders. *J. Clin Psychiatry*, 60 (7):427-435.
3. Kessler, R.C., McGonagle, K.A. (1994). Lifetime prevalence of DSM 3 R psychiatric disorders in the US. *Arch Gen Psychiatry*, 51 (1): 8-19.
4. Wittchen, H.U., Zhao, S., Kessler, R.C. (1994). Generalized Anxiety in the National Comorbidity Survey. *Arch Gen Psychiatry*, 51 (5): 355-364.

5.	Craske, G., Rapee, R., Jackel L. & Barlow, D. (1989). Qualitative dimensions of worry. *Behaviour Research & Therapy*, 27: 397 – 402.

Suggested Reading Anxiety in Divorce

1.	Wehrenberg, M & Prinz, S.M., M.D. (2007). *The anxious brain.* W.W. Norton & Company.
2.	Nutt, D., Rickels, K & Stein, D.(2002). *Generalized Anxiety Disorder.* Martin Dunitz.
3.	*Professional's handbook of psychotropic drugs. (*2001). Springhouse Corporation.
4.	Arana, G.W & Rosenbaum, J.F. (2000). *Handbook of Psychiatric therapy.* Lippincott, W.W.
5.	Rygh, J & Sanderson, W.C. (2004). *Treating Generalised Anxiety Disorder*. The Guilford press.
6.	Leahy, R.L. (2003). *Cognitive Therapy techniques a practitioner's guide.* The Guilford press.
7.	Elkin, A. (1999). *Stress management for dummies.* Wiley Publishing inc.
8.	Westbrook, D., Kennerley, H & Kirk, J. (2008). *An introduction to Cognitive Behaviour Therapy*. Sage Publication.
9.	Weiten, W. (1992). Psychology Themes & variations. Wadsworth: Brooks/Cole Publishing.
10.	Encyclopedia of Mental Health. (1998).Academic Press.
11.	Tallis. (1994). The phenomenology of non-pathological worry; a preliminary investigation. In G. Davey & F. Tallis (eds). *Worrying: perspective on theory, assessment and treatment* (61-89) Chicester, England: John Willey.

TWELVE

Depression and Divorce

"Shared joy is double joy and shared sorrow is half – sorrow".
Swedish proverb

The Purpose

The purpose of this chapter is to explain the manifestation of depression during the divorce context.

Introduction

Depression is a common pathological emotional condition. According to Lepine, depression has a 17% lifetime prevalence among the US and other Western European populations. In a worldwide sample, the average age of the depression onset was 27 years. The data showed that there was a worrying trend of depression developing at a lower age.

The economic burden of depression on the US economy was studied by Greenberg, who found that the annual cost of depression to the US economy is estimated to be $86 billion per annum. Of this staggering amount, $12.4 billion is spent on expenses allocated to cover the costs of hospitalisations, medications and therapists' fees, while an additional $ 24 billion is spent every year on patient absenteeism from work and poor productivity. In addition, a further $8 billion is spent annually on premature death caused by depression-related factors.

Furthermore, the financial impact of depression on the workplace economy is massive. According to Ormel, depressed patients reported eight days of absenteeism from work in the month preceding their visit to primary care facilities.

Data published in 2000 by the world health organisation revealed that depression is the leading cause of disability in the developed world. In addition, the burden caused by depression is second only to respiratory infection, perinatal complications and HIV/Aids. Moreover, it is expected that by the year 2030 the disability caused by depression will be second only to HIV/Aids.

The global increase in the incidence of depression is thought to be partially related to the higher economic hardship prevailing in the developed world which induces higher stress levels. In addition to the elevated stress, the social fabric in modern society has become less supportive and less cohesive, thus further exposing individuals to depression.

It is with little surprise that one discovers that depression is highly prevalent among divorced couples. This high incidence of depression among divorcing couples is due to the additional economic difficulties imposed by the divorce, along with the higher stress levels and reduced support system.

During the divorce, the earliest symptoms of depression to develop are anxiety, insomnia and a sad mood. Usually, these early symptoms of depression develop several weeks before being noticed by the patient and often go untreated. Unfortunately, it is not uncommon to see depressed patients waiting up to six months or even longer before they seek help.

The incidence of depression in the general population is twice as high in women as in men. Furthermore, women in the lower socioeconomic group who also experienced early childhood trauma, physical and sexual abuse and poor parental care, are at the highest risk of developing depression.

It is speculated that exposure to early childhood trauma results in hypersensitivity to future stressors. Such higher sensitivity to future trauma displayed by the abused women is based on studies showing that women with a history of childhood abuse have a six-fold increase in levels of stress hormones, compared to women who have no history of childhood abuse.

The difference of the incidence of depression among the sexes tends to narrow later in life, and after the age of 55 the incidence of depression is equal in both sexes.

Having said that, it is important to understand that for depression to develop, a history of childhood sexual or physical abuse is not required. Similarly, the presence of a history of childhood sexual abuse is not a necessary precursor of depression. The presence of early childhood trauma merely means that women with such a history are at greater risk of becoming depressed during exposure to new stress.

Once established, depression tends to remain chronic, especially without optimal treatment, or if there is no positive change in life circumstances. Moreover, having a depressive episode predisposes the individual to further additional episodes, even when the index episode was successfully treated.

As I mentioned earlier, depression usually develops early in the divorce, pursuant to being exposed to a high level of stress. The early depressive symptoms tend to fluctuate during the day. However, over time, the initial mild symptomatology becomes more serious and more frequent with growing functional impairment.

The occasional sad feeling experienced at the early stage of the illness becomes more intense and frequent. Thoughts of hopelessness, worthlessness and helplessness become more prevalent, along with the increased levels of irritability which are often noticed initially by family members before they become evident to friends and other family members.

In addition to the early psychological symptoms, the physical manifestation of depression becomes more prominent. The physical symptoms of depression involve basic physiological functioning such as appetite, sleep, energy and sex. Over time the physiological symptoms of depression become more prominent, and eventually lead to significant personal, interpersonal, work and leisure impairment.

The cognitive function is also affected by the presence of depression. The normal thought processes become negatively distorted and magnify the negative aspects of the situation, and minimise the positive. Past and present life experiences are perceived negatively, leading to a further loss of interest in any pleasurable activity.

Suicidal ideations become prominent as the depression progresses. According to Black, up to 15% of depressed patients complete suicide. In addition, according to Mallone for every person who completes suicide, 10 other depressed patients have tried, unsuccessfully to end their lives.

According to Gaynes, elderly people aged 65 and above are at 1.5 times a higher risk of committing suicide than their younger counterparts.

According to McIntosh, suicide attempts made by elderly people are more serious, and are associated with more medical complications and death. However, according to Moscick, in the past 30 years, the suicide rates among young adults also rose threefold. These grim statistics highlight the seriousness of depression and its potentially negative impact on these afflicted people as well as on their families. Depression can be highly disabling and a lethal condition, especially in the elderly population.

Risk Factors for Depression

The most common risk factors for depression are:
- Female gender
- Family history of depression
- Lack of support
- Past history of depression
- Present situation of severe stress
- Presence of alcohol and drug abuse
- Death of a close relative
- Marital conflicts and divorce

Studies also showed that the combination of having multiple losses together with feelings of humiliation were more often associated with depression. Moreover, these studies could demonstrate that those spouses whose core role was devalued during a conflict, were much more likely to become depressed. In nasty divorces in which accusations of incompetence are a frequent feature, the chances of developing depression are much higher compared to "happy" divorces which have fewer conflicts, and more mutual respect and co-operation.

What are the Principal Depressive Symptoms?

Depression is a mental illness that affects emotions, cognition, many bodily physiological processes, and which ultimately leads to personal, social and work impairment. The depressive symptoms can be divided into three principal domains:
- Emotional domain
- Cognitive domain
- Physiological domain

A.   *Emotional symptoms*; the emotional symptoms of depression are low moods and a pervasive feeling of sadness, irritability, tension and anxiety. The emotional symptoms tend to develop early at the onset of the illness.

B.   *Cognitive symptoms*: the cognitive processes during the depressive state become negatively distorted. Pessimistic views regarding past events, present life circumstances and the future are highly prominent. The past, the present and forthcoming events are negatively viewed, while the positive aspects are overlooked.

Thoughts of death and suicide are a frequent feature of the depressive state. In severe cases, paranoid ideations can further aggravate the course of the illness. Furthermore, even normal physical symptoms such as headache or back pain can be falsely interpreted as a symptom of a terminal condition such as incurable cancer. The psychotic interpretation of normal physiological phenomena can lead to uncharacteristically strange behaviour. Delusions of poverty can be a further sign of the serious deterioration that depression can cause. These deluded patients falsely believe they are destitute, despite being presented with contrary evidence.

Another cognitive feature of depression is reduced concentration. Early minor memory lapses due to reduced focus and concentration can further deteriorate into serious short-term memory impairment which can seriously affect functionality.

Loss of interest in personal and social activities is also a common feature of depression which limits social interaction and involvement in other leisure activities.

C.   *Physiological symptoms*: the physiological symptoms of depression develop early. Sleep difficulties include an inability to fall asleep or to maintain sleep. Sleep is severely interrupted during the night, and waking up earlier than intended is highly common. The overall sleep quality becomes poor.

Energy levels become extremely low and are associated with tiredness, which further alienates the depressed person from social interactions and promotes avoidance behaviour. Appetite is markedly affected during the depressive state. There is either an increase in, or more frequently decreased appetite with a significant weight gain or weight loss. The ingested food becomes tasteless, and in severe cases, there is a total loss of appetite. The sex drive also becomes an unfortunate victim of depression often accompanied by an inability to experience orgasm. Reduced libido is often aggravated by antidepressant medication and should be carefully addressed by the therapist. The full range of the depressive symptomatology is illustrated in Table 12.1.

Table 12.1   The Depressive Symptoms:

Emotional symptoms	Cognitive symptoms	Physiological symptoms
•Depressed mood	•suicidal thoughts	•fatigue
•irritability	•thought of hurting others	•sleep problems
•apathy	•excessive worry	•decreased appetite
•nervousness	•pessimism	•weight loss
•indecisiveness	•excessive guilt	•sexual impairment
•hypersensitivity to criticism	• negative cognitive distortion	•orgasmic difficulties
•hoplessness	•hypocondriacal tendencies	•back pains
•worthlessness	•reduced self esteem	•headache
•helplessness	•reduced concentration	•muscular pain
•anger outbursts	•crying spells	•muscle tension
•reduced leisure activities	•excessive dependency on others	•heart palpitation
•reduced social involvement	•paranoia	•heartburn
•lack of interest	•delusion of poverty	•gastro intestinal upset
	•delusion of having incurable disease	

The Course of the Depressive Illness

Depression, if untreated, can continue relentlessly and may become chronic with devastating personal and interpersonal implications. The average length of an untreated depression is nine months, while treated depression can take up to three months to achieve full recovery. Early treatment discontinuation invariably results in relapse, which further highlights the importance of getting optimal and appropriate treatment as early as possible.

Unfortunately, even successfully treated depressive patients can experience additional relapses while on medication. In addition, studies show that the recurrence of depression can be up to 60% in the first five years after treatment cessation of a first depressive episode. On the other hand, in patients having experienced more than two depressive episodes, there is a 70% increased probability of having a third one. Depressed patients who have had three or more episodes are 90% guaranteed to experience more of the same.

There is a large body of evidence reported by Piccinelli to suggest that the longer the depressive state continues, the more likely it is to persist. Coryll also found that patients who did not recover from a depressive episode within the first two months, had a one in three chance of recovery over the next two months, and a one in six chance during the following eight months. Furthermore, the steady decline in symptom improvement can reach only a 7% response rate in the second year in untreated depressive patients.

Depression is considered chronic whenever the depressive symptoms continue longer than two years regardless of receiving treatment. According to Fochtmann, the most common predictors of a chronic depressive course are:

• 	Having a family history of depression
• 	Experiencing multiple losses

- The presence of an additional chronic medical illness
- The presence of substance dependence
- Work impairment, unemployment.
- Having financial difficulties

Depression experienced during the divorce further complicates matters, and reduces the possibility of reaching a satisfactory and productive divorce outcome, as depression distorts cognition and increases ambivalence, dependency and poor decision-making. In addition, the low motivation and the reduced energy will affect any positive initiatives, and also affects decision-making leading to poor legal and financial management.

Due to the devastating effects of depression on functionality and on decision-making, it is highly important to have a quick and early evaluation in order to detect the presence of depression.

Are You Depressed?

Although it is very unwise to make a self-diagnosis of depression, you don't have to be a rocket scientist or a specialist psychiatrist to make a provisional diagnosis of depression. Look at Table 12.1 and try to identify any symptoms listed in the table which sound familiar to you. If you have experienced any of the depressive symptoms listed in the table in the past two weeks then proceed to Table 12.2. and write them down.

Table 12.2   **Your Depressive Symptoms**

Emotional symptoms	Cognitive symptoms	Physiological symptoms
• _____	• _____	• _____
• _____	• _____	• _____
• _____	• _____	• _____
• _____	• _____	• _____
• _____	• _____	• _____
• _____	• _____	• _____

Early detection of depression is highly important. Table 12.3 includes the most prominent depressive symptoms and measures their severity.

Daily assessment of your depressive symptom severity is an essential step in order to be able to monitor the treatment progress.

Table 12.3   Depression Evaluation and Monitoring: DEM.

Symptoms level		Unhappy mood	Sleep problems	Appetite problems	Reduced energy
No symptoms	0				
Feel minimal symptoms	1				
Mild symptoms	2				
Moderate symptoms	3				
Panicking	4				
Daily Total score					

Dr Shlomo Brook

Symptoms level		Reduced concentration	Reduced sex drive	Tension	Irritability
No symptoms	0				
Feel minimal symptoms	1				
Mild symptoms	2				
Moderate symptoms	3				
Panicking	4				
Daily Total score					

Symptoms level		Loss interest in social interaction	Suicidal ideations	Hopeless & worthless	Feel guilty
No symptoms	0				
Feel minimal symptoms	1				
Mild symptoms	2				
Moderate symptoms	3				
Panicking	4				
Daily Total score					

Total daily depressive score	Day 1	Day 2	Day 3	Day 4	Day 5	Day 6	Day 7

Interpretation of your depression score:

Score	Interpretation
0 - 12	*Normal mood range:* You can experience minimal depressive symptoms that have no impact on your day to day functions.
13 - 24	*Mild depression:* You experience some symptoms that can cause minimal distress.
25 - 37	*Moderate depression:* Symptoms may cause some distress
38 - 48	*Severe depression:* Symptoms can lead to a high level of distress and can be incapacitating

Achieving a constant high score requires an urgent consultation with a health care professional, especially in the presence of prominent suicidal ideas. A low score indicates the presence of a mild depressive state which can initially be controlled by psychological interventions such as cognitive behavioural therapy (CBT).

What Causes Depression?

The Biological Theory of Depression

Although the exact etiology of depression is still unknown, it is widely speculated that depression is the final step of a complex interaction between several biological, psychological and social factors. In simple words, depression develops pursuant to a genetic predisposition which is further induced by social and psychological factors. This bio-psycho-social theory of depression is further illustrated in Figure 12.4.

Figure 12.4   The Biological Causes of Depression

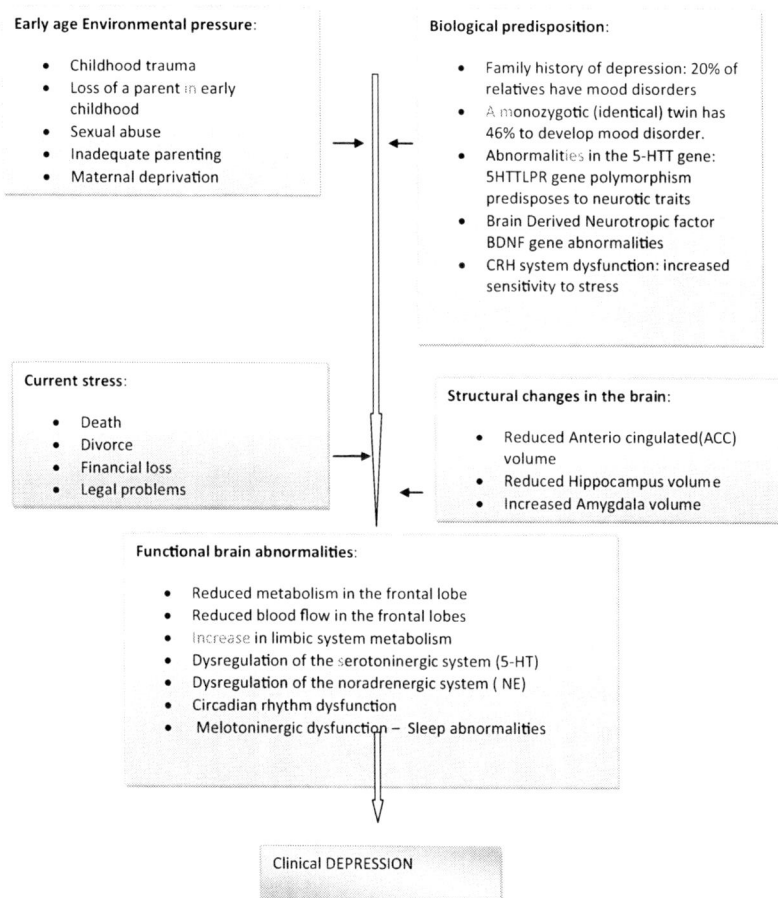

Early age Environmental pressure:

- Childhood trauma
- Loss of a parent in early childhood
- Sexual abuse
- Inadequate parenting
- Maternal deprivation

Biological predisposition:

- Family history of depression: 20% of relatives have mood disorders
- A monozygotic (identical) twin has 46% to develop mood disorder.
- Abnormalities in the 5-HTT gene: 5HTTLPR gene polymorphism predisposes to neurotic traits
- Brain Derived Neurotropic factor BDNF gene abnormalities
- CRH system dysfunction: increased sensitivity to stress

Current stress:

- Death
- Divorce
- Financial loss
- Legal problems

Structural changes in the brain:

- Reduced Anterio cingulated(ACC) volume
- Reduced Hippocampus volume
- Increased Amygdala volume

Functional brain abnormalities:

- Reduced metabolism in the frontal lobe
- Reduced blood flow in the frontal lobes
- Increase in limbic system metabolism
- Dysregulation of the serotoninergic system (5-HT)
- Dysregulation of the noradrenergic system (NE)
- Circadian rhythm dysfunction
- Melotoninergic dysfunction – Sleep abnormalities

Clinical DEPRESSION

Dr Shlomo Brook

The Psychological Theories for Depression

The Psychodynamic View

The first psychodynamic theory for depression was developed by Sigmund Freud in 1917. This theory was based on Freud's observations of the similarities between depression and grief reactions in those individuals who suffered the loss of a loved one.

According to Freud, an unconscious process starts after the death of a loved one which results in a psychological regression to the oral phase. The oral phase as described by Freud is an early developmental psychological stage in the child's development, and is characterised by the presence of complete dependency. The result of such a psychological regression to an early developmental phase is a merger of the mourner's identity with that of the diseased loved one.

This introjection process results in the redirection of previously existing feelings of anger toward the deceased inwards, towards oneself, thus causing depression. Despite such an appealing and sophisticated hypothesis, there are many individuals who suffer from depression without having experienced actual loss. To overcome this problem, Freud proposed that the loss can either be actual or imaginary. Thus the depressed do not have to experience a real loss; instead, they can create a symbolic mental alternative representation of an imaginary loss. Several studies conducted on monkeys which had been separated from their mothers discovered that the separated monkeys exhibit behaviour similar to depression, thus indirectly confirming Freud's hypothesis.

Another study conducted by Rene Spitz in 1946 on infants separated from their mothers and placed in a nursery discovered that the separated infants became weepy, sad and withdrew from the environment. Spitz called such behaviour anaclitic depression.

As attractive as the psychodynamic theories are, only less than 10% of all people who experience loss become depressed, thus leaving the other 90% without a plausible explanation.

The Behavioural View

Behavioural theorists believe that depression develops pursuant to a change in the number of rewards and punishments people experience during their lives. According to this theory, developed by Lewinsohn in the early 1990s, people's positive rewards dwindle over time, leading to these people exhibiting less constructive behaviour. As the positive rewards decline, the action of less constructive behaviour leads such people to spiral towards depression. Studies conducted by Lewinsohn showed that the amount of rewards people obtain in their lives are related to the presence or absence of depression.

The depressed subjects reported having fewer positive rewards than the non-depressed individuals, and their depression improved when their rewards increased. Similar recent studies have found a strong correlation between positive life events and having greater life satisfaction and happiness.

The critics of the behavioural theory maintain that although depressed people experience more adverse life events, it may be possible that their original depressed mood is conducive to their reduced social rewards and not otherwise.

The Cognitive View

Cognitive theorists believe that people with depression have a distorted negative view of the world which, in turn, is the cause of their depression.

Cognitive behavioural theory was developed by A.T Beck in the early sixties, and still occupies a prominent role in the etiology of depression and its treatment.

According to Beck, the negative thought process lies at the heart of the depressive state. In simple words, we feel the way we think. If you think negatively, you will feel unhappy and depressed. According to Beck, depressed people resort to a prominent negative cognitive distortion comprised of excessive negative core beliefs, dysfunctional assumptions and excessive use of negative automatic thoughts.

Since the initial observations made by Beck and his associates, numerous studies confirm the association between depression and the presence of the maladaptive, distorted cognitive thought process. However, most studies fail to show whether the presence of cognitive dysfunction is the cause of depression, or whether it is the result of the depressive process.

Learned Helplessness

According to Seligman's theory published in 1975, depression develops as the result of having an excessive feeling of helplessness. People become depressed when they believe that they no longer have control of their lives or the situation. Numerous studies show that animals exposed to adverse hopeless situations develop behaviour similar to that exhibited during depression. The helpless animals lose interest in their surroundings and their social interaction. Studies on humans exposed to uncontrolled negative event scenarios, tend to score higher on depressive surveys.

The Social Views

The incidence of depression is substantially different among society's sub-groups. A woman has a much higher incidence of depression than a man. Similarly, the risk of depression is much higher in those individuals residing in public buildings. A study conducted by Bazargan in 2005 on Hispanic and African Americans showed that depression was higher in those living in poverty, belonging to big families and with more health problems. The lack of social support influences the likelihood of subjects developing depression. Another study conducted by Weissman in 1991 showed that divorced and separated people had three times the rate of depression of married people. Weisman's results are illustrated further in Figure 12.5.

Figure 12.5: **Rates of depression and marital status (Adapted from Weismann 1991).**

Rates of depression& marital status

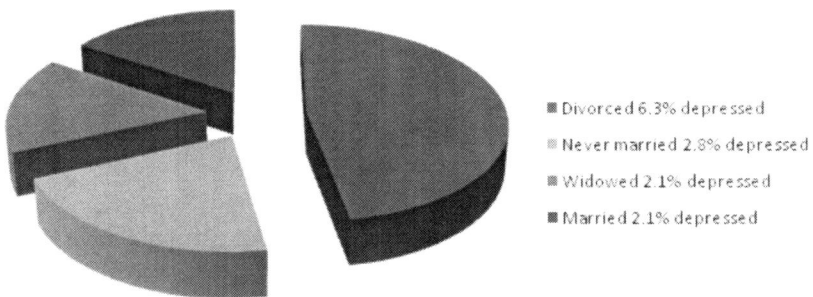

- Divorced 6.3% depressed
- Never married 2.8% depressed
- Widowed 2.1% depressed
- Married 2.1% depressed

Another social study conducted by Moos in 1999, showed that depressed people with limited social support remain depressed longer than those who have a supportive spouse or strong friendships.

The following vignette illustrates the role of divorce in depression.

John is a 43 year old man. He held a high position in an insurance company and was happily married for 20 years to Jane. John's life took a terrible twist one day when he came home early from work to find his wife in bed with his best friend. From that moment the life he had known changed forever. His wife took their two children and moved out of the family home along with their dog. Initially, John tried to hide the situation from his family and his work colleagues. He continued to work during the day and returned to his empty home at night. However, within days his colleagues noticed a change in his behaviour. John became irritable and short-tempered with his subordinates, he often forgot to present a required task and needed to be constantly reminded by his loyal secretary. He avoided his close friends and declined offers to attend their regular golf days. John found the nights long and depressing. He had difficulty falling asleep and needed some alcohol to help him sleep. However, he often woke up at 2 a.m. and had to spend the rest of the night watching boring T.V with the false comfort of strong liquour as he could not fall asleep. The morning was very upsetting as John was extremely tired and was looking for an excuse not to go to work. Often he stayed in bed, did not shower, and left the house in a total mess. He lost weight as he had no appetite and avoided anything that reminded him of happiness as he felt that he did not deserve to be happy. He blamed himself for the situation and started to believe that death was the only solution to the situation. One day after his ex-wife refused to allow him to talk to his children; he went to the local pharmacy, bought a pack of over- the-counter painkillers and swallowed them all along with half a bottle of strong liquor. His sister, who accidentally stopped by for a surprise visit, found him in a confused state and rushed him to the local Emergency room.

In addition to the unpleasant nature of depression, the illness has a severe impact on many aspects of the person's life. During the early phase, the depressive symptoms are mild, and have a limited impact on the level of functioning. However, as the depression becomes more prominent it significantly interferes with daily activities.

Depression reduces self-esteem and personal confidence, while it increases ambivalence and social withdrawal. Interpersonal relationships become maladaptive, affecting communication and interaction with significant others.

A depressed parent going through divorce often displays a maladaptive interactional style with his/her children and with the ex-spouse leading to multiple conflicts, unnecessary frictions, misunderstanding and disappointment.

A survey which Princeton Research Associates conducted in 1996, as illustrated in Figure 12.6 showed that depressed parents are less likely to play with, read to, or hug their children, and are more likely to get frustrated and yell at their children compared to non-depressed parents.

Figure 12.6 Princeton Survey Research Associates, 1996 (Adapted) on how depressed and non-depressed parents interact with their children

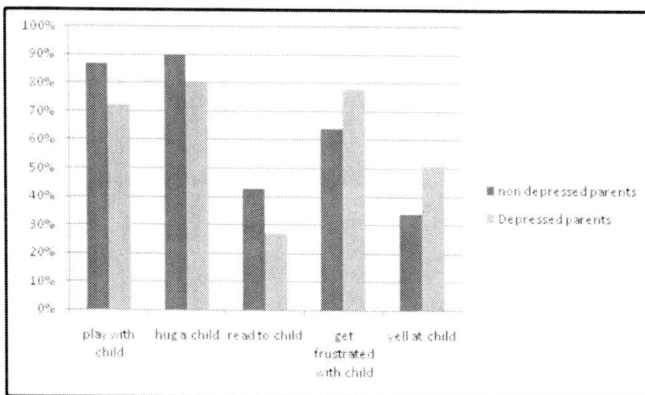

The negative effect of depression on the personal, interpersonal and vocational life warrants a quick intervention which will bring a fast recovery and improved functionality which often translates into a smoother and more effective divorce process.

Key Points

• Depression is a highly common condition affecting one in seven people.
• Depression is associated with psychological, emotional, physiological and behavioural symptoms.
• Depression is associated with severe functional impairment.
• Depression is associated with high mortality rates. Suicide is the leading cause of death affecting 15% of depressed patients.
• Depression is highly common in divorce and often has a negative impact on the divorce process.

Depression in Divorce References and Suggested Readings

1. Lepine, J.P., Gastpar, M., Mendlewicz, J., Tylee, A. (1997). Depression in the community: the first pan-European study DEPRES. *Int Clin Psychopharmacol*, 12 (1): 19-29.
2. Greenberg, P.E., Leon, S.A., Birnbaum, H.G. (2001). Cost of Depression: Current assessment and future directions. *Expert Rev Pharmacoeconomic Outcomes Res*, 1:89-96.
3. Simon, G.E., in Korff, M., Barlow, W. (1995). Health care costs of primary care patients with depression. *Arch Gen Psychiatry*, 52(10):850-856.

4.   Ormel, J., Von kroff, M., Ustum T.B. (1994). Common mental disorders and disability across cultures. Results from the WHO Collaborative study. *JAMA*, 272(22):1741-1748.

5.   Black, D.W., Winokur, G. (1990). Suicide and psychiatric diagnosis. In Blumenthal, S.J., Kupfer, D.J. (eds). *Suicide over life cycle.* Washington DC: American Psychiatric Press.

6.   Malone, K.M., Hass, G.L., Sweeney, J.A. (1995). Major Depression and the risk of attempted suicide. *J Affect Dis,* 34: 173-185.

7.   Gaynes, B.N., Wes, S.L. (2004). Screening for suicide risk in adults. *Ann Intern Med,* 140:822-835.

8.   McIntosh, J.L. (1995). Suicide prevention in the elderly. *Suicide Life Threat Behav,* 25: 180-192.

9.   Moscicki, E.K. (1995). Epidemiology of suicidal behaviour. *Suicide Life Threat Behav,* 25: 22- 35.

10.   Piccinelli, M. Wilkinson, G. (1994). Outcome of depression in psychiatric setting. *Br J. Psy,* 164:297-304.

11.   Coryell, W. (1991). Predictors of relapse into major depressive disorder in a non-clinical population. *Am. J. Psy,* 148: 1353-1358.

12.   Fochtmann, L.J. (1994). Animal studies of ect: Foundation for future research. *Pshychopharmacology Bull,* 30:321-344.

13.   Shea, M.T., Elkin. (1988). Psychotherapeutic treatment of depression in American Psychiatric Press review of Psychiatry. In A.J. Frances and R.E. Hales (eds). *Washington DC APP,* 1988: 235-255.

14.   Hollon, S.D. (1992). Cognitive therapy and pharmacotherapy for depression singly and in combination. *Arch Gen psychiatry,* 49:774-78.

15.   Kahn, A., Warner, H.A. (2000). Symptom reduction and suicide risk in patients treated with placebo in antidepressant clinical trial. *Arc Gen Psychiatry,* 57: 311-317.

16.   Brenner, R. (2000). Comparison of an extract of hypericum and sertraline in the treatment of depression: a double blind randomized

pilot study. *Clin Ther,* 22:411-419.

17. Schrader, E. (2000). Equivalence of SJW extract (ze117 and fluoxetine: a randomized controlled study in mild – moderate depression). *Int Clin Psychopharmacology,* 15:61-68.

18. Schulz, V. (2001). Rational phytotherapy: a physician guide to herbal medicine. (4th ed.).Berlin: Springer.

19. Spillman, M., Fava, M. Sadenosyl-Methionine in psychiatric disorders. *CNSb Drugs,* 6:416 – 425.

20. Lands, W.E.M. (1992). Biochemistry and physiology of fatty acids. *FASEB J,* 6:2530-2536.

21. Levine. (1999). Combination of inositol and SSRI in the treatment of depression. *Biol. Psychiatry,* 45:270-273.

22. Potokar, J., Thase, M. (2003). *Advances in the management and treatment of depression.* Martin Dunitz.

23. Freud, S. (1933). *New introductory lectures on psychoanalysis.* New York: Norton.

24. Bazargan, M. (2005) Treatment of self-reported depression among Hispanic and African Americans. J. *Hlt care poor underserved,* 16: 328 – 344.

25. Seligman, M. (2005). Positive psychology progress: empirical validation of interventions. *Amer. Psychologist,* 60(5): 410 – 421.

26. Beck, A.T. (1979). *Cognitive theory of depression.* New York: Guilford Press.

27. World Health Organisation. (2004). Prevalence severity and unmet need for treatment of mental disorders in the world health organization world mental health surveys. *JAMA* 291, (21): 2581 – 2590.

28. Weissman, M. (200). Social functioning and the treatment of depression. *J.Clin. Psychiatry,* 61, supplement: 33 – 38.

29. Weissman, M. (1992). The changing rate of major depression: cross national comparisons. Cross national collaborative group. *JAMA,* 268 (21): 3098 – 3105.

30.   Stern magazine. (2004). Survey. *Stern Magazine*, July 23, 2004.

31.   Moos, R.H. (1999). Symptom-based predictors of a 10 year chronic course of treated depression. *J. Nerv. Ment. Dis.*, 187 (6): 360 – 368.

32.   Princeton Survey Research Associates. (1996). *Healthy steps for young children: Survey of parents.* Princeton: Author.

THIRTEEN

Antidepressant Treatment of Depression

"God heals and the doctor takes the fees".
Benjamin Franklin, in Poor Richard's Almanac, 1736

The Purpose

The purpose of this chapter is to explain the pharmacological treatment modalities available for depression.

Introduction

Over the past 50 years antidepressants have become the principal treatment modality for moderate to severe cases of depression. The effectiveness of antidepressants in the treatment of depressive states was established by thousand of clinical studies conducted during the last 50 years. However, their clinically proven effectiveness is somewhat limited by their bothering side-effects, dangerousness in overdose and by the stigma associated with their use.

The first mood-elevating medicine was Iproniazid, which was a medication used for the treatment of Tuberculosis. Iproniazid improved the depressive symptoms of T.B patients, probably due to its irreversible inhibitory effects on the Monoamine Oxidase (MAOI) which is an important enzyme involved with the metabolism of Serotonin, Dopamine and Noradrenaline. Despite its promising efficacy in improving the depressive state, Iproniazid usage was abandoned due to its unpleasant and severe side-effect profile.

Iproniazid was substituted in the late 1950s with a new class of medications belong to the Tricyclic family. The Tricyclic medications showed a promising efficacy in the treatment of depression, due to their somewhat better tolerability profile compared to the Iproniazid. The Tricyclics' effectiveness was due to their ability to modulate the brain's Serotonin and Noradrenline levels which are currently believed to be the principal neurotransmitters involved in depression.

Soon after their discovery, the Tricyclics gained a wide popularity among therapists, and they extensively dominated the psycho-pharmacological market despite their unpleasant side-effect profile and their poor safety record in overdose, as well as their complicated use.

The first generation of Tricyclics was soon replaced by a second and third generation which had a somewhat slightly better side-effect profile. Imipramine and amitriptyline which were the first TCAs are still widely used, especially in developing countries due to their low price. Their extensive use backed by the World Health Organisation, despite their side-effect profile which includes a dry mouth, constipation and effects on the heart conduction has helped to reduce depressive symptoms and improve functionality significantly.

The latest generation of the TCA family was Lofepramine which has a better safety profile, especially in overdose, as well as a slightly better side-effect profile.

The 1980s revolutionised the antidepressant scene with the introduction of Fluoxetine. Fluoxetine was the first member of a new antidepressant class known as the SSRI (Serotonin reuptake inhibitors). The SSRI class name derived from their pharmacological action. The SSRI selectively blocks the brain's serotonin re-uptake leading to a higher serotonin level available at the space between the nerve cells.

The SSRI class produced five representatives which gained vast popularity and dominated the antidepressant market for more than 20 years. The high popularity of the SSRI was the result of a massive media campaign combined with a somewhat better side-effect profile.

Over the past several years, newer generations of antidepressants have been developed, probably due to the unmet need of the depressive treatment which includes faster and better action, less side-effects and better safety in overdose.

The newer antidepressants were classified according to their mode of action, and include the SNRI family with Selective Serotonin and Noradrenaline's re-uptake inhibitory effects. This family is comprised of two members, Venlafaxin and Duloxetine. The NARI class is another newly developed antidepressant with a principal Noradrenergic re-uptake inhibitor effect. The NARI class comprises the Reboxetine as the principal representative. The NaSSa is one of the newest classes with a principal Noradrenergic and a specific Serotonergic receptor enhancer activity. The principal and only representative of this class is Mirtazapine.

The newer generation was initially considered to work faster, and to have a better and improved side-effect profile and to be safer in overdose compared to the SSRI class. However, clinical practice showed that all the newer antidepressants classes also have side-effects which do not substantially differ from those of the previously developed SSRI products. Moreover, all antidepressant medications proved to have similar efficacy, and to require at least two to four weeks before users showed any clinical improvement.

A survey conducted by Wallis and published in Time in 2005 found that, despite the huge progress in the treatment of depression, most patients preferred other activities to improve their mood. The survey results are illustrated in Figure 13.1.

Figure 13.1   What people do to improve their mood, adapted from Wallis, 2005.

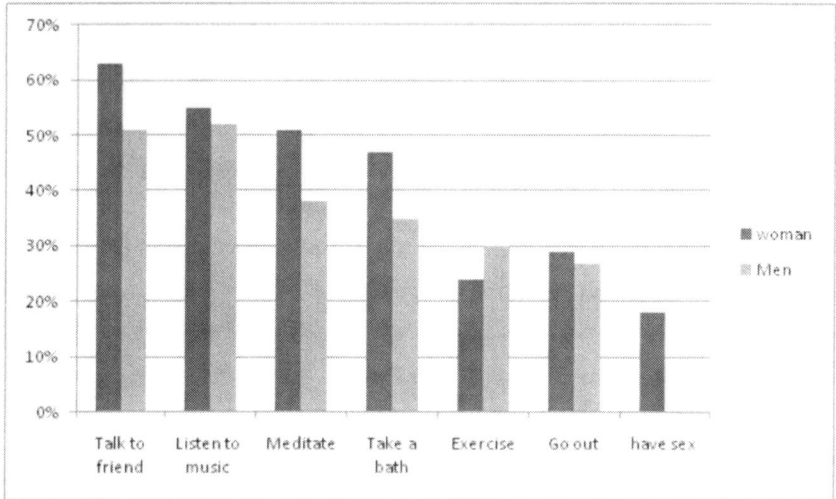

Wallis, C. (2005). The new science of happiness. *Time,* 165 (3), January 17, 2005, A2 – A9.

Regarding the mechanism of action of most antidepressants, there are still wide gaps in the current knowledge about the precise mode of action of all antidepressants, and the latency in their onset of action.

The Antidepressant Mechanism of Action

Although the actual therapeutic effect of the antidepressants is not entirely known, it is widely believed that most antidepressants exert their clinical antidepressant properties through their effect on the Dopaminergic,

Noradrenergic and the Serotoninergic systems.

All antidepressants facilitate the neurotransmitter activity at their corresponding post-synaptic neuron receptor sites by blocking the neurotransmitter reuptake receptors. This complicated concept is illustrated in Figure 13.2.

Figure 13.2   Antidepressant Postulated Action

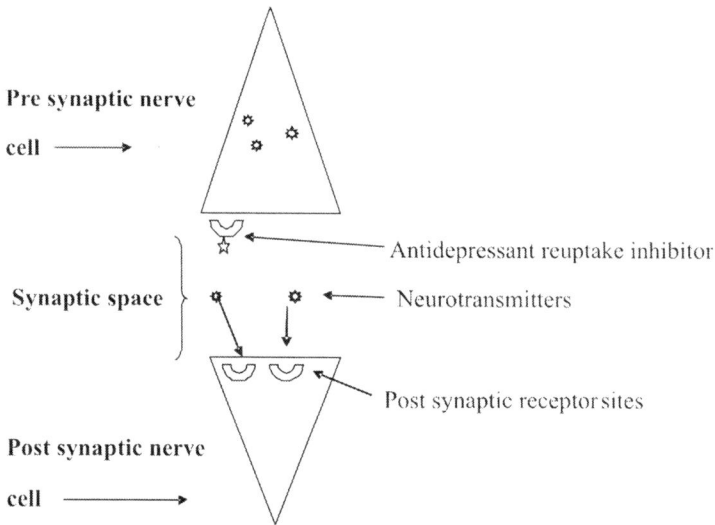

The principal monoamine neurotransmitters involved in depression are Serotonin, Noradrenaline and Dopamine. These three neurotransmitters are involved with mood regulation.

The principal functions of these three neurotransmitters are illustrated in Figure 13.3.

Figure 13.3   The Psychological Effects of Dopamine, Serotonin and Noradrenaline

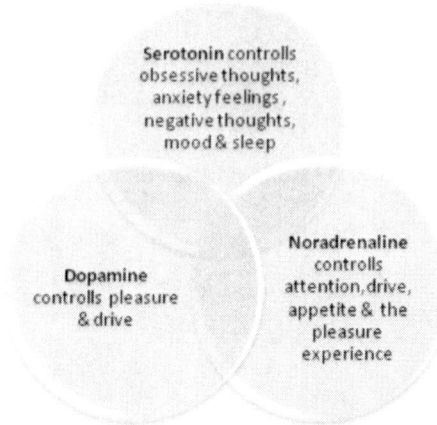

Serotonin controlls
obsessive thoughts,
anxiety feelings,
negative thoughts,
mood & sleep

Dopamine
controlls pleasure
& drive

Noradrenaline
controlls
attention, drive,
appetite & the
pleasure
experience

The Clinical Use of Antidepressants

Antidepressants are principally used for the treatment of moderate to severe depression. All antidepressants have at least a two week delay before there is any noticeable mood change.

The peak antidepressant effect becomes evident after two to four months of continuous treatment. Early treatment termination is usually followed by a depressive relapse especially if treatment was stopped within the first 16 weeks of therapy. Treatment responders need to continue with antidepressant treatment for a minimum period of six months in order to minimise the possibility of a relapse.

Moreover, recent research has shown that continuous prophylactic treatment with antidepressants can prevent new depressive episodes for up to five years of regular treatment at doses equal to that of the acute phase.

Unfortunately, up to 20% of patients can experience an acute depressive relapse despite ongoing treatment with antidepressants.

The pharmacological treatment of depression involves three overlapping phases:

The acute, the continuation phase and the maintenance phase are illustrated in Figure 13.4.

Figure 13.4   The Treatment Phases of Depression

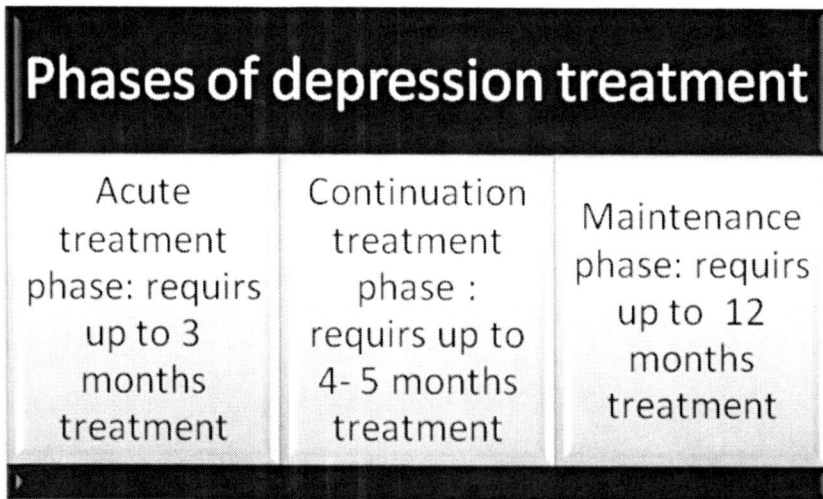

Phases of depression treatment

Acute treatment phase: requirs up to 3 months treatment	Continuation treatment phase : requirs up to 4- 5 months treatment	Maintenance phase: requirs up to 12 months treatment

Currently there is sufficient evidence to suggest that long term usage of antidepressants can significantly reduce the risk of developing depressive recurrence, as well as improving the patients' quality of life and their level of functioning.

In long-term antidepressant studies, the risk of recurrence was 60% in the patients' group which stopped treatment, in comparison to only 19% recurrence of depression in the patient's group which used antidepressants for 12 months after recovery. Furthermore, in patients with a history of more than four depressive episodes, the risk for recurrence was 3.3% per week in comparison with a 1% weekly risk for those patients who had experienced only one depressive episode.

All antidepressants share the following properties:

- All currently available antidepressants have 60 % efficacy rates in the treatment of depression.
- All currently available antidepressants require at least one to three weeks continuous use to indicate a response.
- Psycho-education and early communication of the possible side-effects of the prescribed drug can improve compliance.
- Most antidepressants' side-effects are temporary and resolve within a few days of treatment.
- Serious side-effects require substitution of the medicine with another product preferably from a different class.
- Abrupt discontinuation of antidepressants can cause discontinuation symptoms and a recurrence of depressive symptoms.
- The addition of psychological interventions such as CBT improves the overall prognosis and improves treatment compliance.

The most current widely used antidepressant classes are summarised in Table 13.5.

13.5   The Principal Available Antidepressants

MAOI class	Tricyclic class	Tetracyclic class	SSRI class
Phenelzine	Amitriptyline	Maprotiline	Fluoxetine
Trancycpromine	Clomipramine	Mianserine	Fluvoxamine
	Imipramine	Trazadone	Sertraline
	Trimipramine		Paroxetine
	Dotiepine		Citalopram
	lofepramine		Es citalopram
SNRI class	**NARI class**	**NaSSA class**	**Dopamine class**
Venlafaxine	Reboxetine	Mirtazapine	Welbutrin
Duloxetine			

The NICE guidelines published in 2004 suggest that initially, SSRIs should be the first line of treatment for depression because they are as effective as TCAs, and their use is less likely to be discontinued due to their favourable side-effect profile.

The Discontinuation Syndrome

The abrupt discontinuation of antidepressants can lead to severe withdrawal symptoms which can develop within one to three days of treatment cessation. The discontinuation symptoms usually disappear within one day if previous treatment commences. However, permanent treatment cessation can prolong the discontinuation symptoms which can last for between one to three weeks.

Discontinuation syndrome appears to be more common with the SSRI medication. Paroxetine and fluvoxamine have a higher propensity to cause discontinuation due to their shorter half-life and the absence of active metabolites. Fluoxetine and Sertraline have a lower propensity to cause a discontinuation syndrome due to their long half-life and the presence of active metabolites.

Although the discontinuation syndrome was widely described with the SSRI, it is also observed with the old TCAs as well as with the other newer generations of antidepressants. The principal symptoms of the discontinuation syndrome are summarised in Table 13.6.

Table 13.6   The Discontinuation Symptoms

Discontinuation symptoms

Physical: flu like symptoms, excessive sweating, nausea, vomiting,Chills,	**Psychiatric**: anxiety, insomnia, nightmares irritability, Fatigue	**Neurological**; tremor, dizziness, headache,Myalgia

In order to avoid discontinuation symptoms, it is advisable to gradually reduce the antidepressants' use over the period of a month.

The properties of the most commonly used antidepressant are summarised in the following tables:

A) TCA
Table 13.7   Clomipramine

How supplied	Cap. 25mg, 75mg	Daily dose	Start 25mg a day, increase within 2 weeks to a max. of 150 mg/day in divided doses
Action	1. Selective inhibition of re-uptake of serotonin in the CNS 2. Possible post-synaptic blockade of Dopamine receptors	**Precautions**	1. Urine retention 2. Glaucoma 3. Impaired kidney, liver 4. Hyperthyroidism 5. Convulsions 6. Alcohol use 7. Safety in breast-feeding unclear 8. May activate Mania
Indication	1. Depression 2. OCD	**Contraindication**	1 Previous use of MAOI within 14 days 2. Acute MI 3. Hypersensitivity to the drug
Absorption	Well absorbed in the GI tract.	**Metabolism**	1. Liver. Has 1 active metabolite desmethyl-clomipramine
Excretion	Urine 66% Faeces 44%	**Half-life**	36 hours for parent drug 69 hours for metabolite

Tips for use	1. Take drug with food to minimise GI A/E		
	2. Use sugarless candy for dry mouth		
	3. Recommend use of effective contraceptive		
	4. Recommend use of high fibre diet for constipation		
	5. Avoid hazardous activities		

| Side-Effect | Frequency | | Stop the drug immediately |
	Common	**Rare**	
Constipation	√		
Dry mouth	√		
Anorexia	√		
Dizziness	√		
Tremor		√	
Hypotension	√		
Seizure		√	√
Palpitations		√	
Weight gain	√		
Delayed Ejaculation		√	
Myalgia		√	
Decreased Libido	√		

Table 13.8   TCA - Imipramine

How supplied	Tab. 10mg 25mg, 50mg	Daily dose	Start 75mg a day, increase within 2 weeks to a max. of 200 mg/day in divided doses
Action	1. Inhibiting re-uptake of noradrenaline and serotonine in the CNS at the pre-synaptic neurons	**Precautions**	1. Urine retention 2. Glaucoma 3. Impaired kidney, liver 4. Hyperthyroidism 5. Convulsions 6. Alcohol use 7. Safety in breast-feeding unclear 8. Secreted in milk 9. May activate Mania
Indication	1. Depression 2. Enuresis	**Contraindication**	1 Previous use of MAOI within 14 days. 2. Acute MI 3. Hypersensitivity to the drug 4. Narrow angle glaucoma
Absorption	1. Rapidly absorbed in the GI tract. 2. Plasma peak 30 min – 2 H	**Metabolism**	1. Liver. Has 1 active metabolite desipramine
Excretion	Urine mostly	**Steady state**	2 – 5 days

Tips for use	1. Take drug with food to minimise GI A/E 2. Use sugarless candy for dry mouth 3. Sun exposure may cause hypersensitivity 4. Recommend use of high fibre diet for constipation 5. Avoid hazardous activities		
Side-Effect	**Frequency** **Common**	**Rare**	Stop the drug immediately
Constipation	√		
Dry mouth	√		
Blurred vision	√		
Urine retention		√	√
Anorexia/ abdominal cramps	√		
Dizziness	√		
Arrhythmias/ heart block		√	√
Hypotension	√		
Seizure		√	√
Palpitations		√	

Weight gain	√		
Delayed Ejaculation		√	
CVA		√	√
Decreased Libido	√		
Galactor-rhea		√	

B)   The Selective Serotonin Reuptake Inhibitor (SSRI)

Since the SSRIs are the most prescribed antidepressants in developed countries, their mode of action and side-effect profile merit a more comprehensive discussion.

Fluoxetine was the first SSRI to be introduced in 1988 to the antidepressant market, and it quickly gained massive popularity due to the major media coverage and huge publicity. Fluoxetine was, at some point considered to be the "magic pill" which would change the life of millions. Fluoxetine's use is a simple and requires the ingestion of one tablet a day, and it is considered to be relatively safe in overdose. The result of the Fluoxetine popularity and the huge revenues it made prompted the quick development of other SSRIs, which happily joined the antidepressant market. Currently there are five SSRI medications on the market. All SSRIs demonstrated comparable efficacy and showed that they were significantly better than the placebos, and could prevent depressive relapse for up to one year of treatment.

All SSRIs have equal efficacy for the treatment of depression. In addition, there is little evidence to show a positive correlation between SSRI dose increase and faster or better antidepressant effects.

However, despite their similar mode of action each SSRI has a different side-effect profile which is summarised in Table 13.9.

Table 13.9   The Principal Side-Effects of SSRI

Gastrointestinal	Characteristics	Psychiatric	Characteristics
Nausea	Gastro intestinal effects are the most common side-effects of SSRIs. However, they are often transient and dose-related	Nervousness	Appear early and subside within 3 weeks
Loss of appetite		Anxiety	
Diarrhoea		Agitation	
Gastro-intestinal bleeding	Can be increased three-fold	Headache	In 30%
		Weight gain	In some individuals
Anticholinergic	**Characteristics**	Sweating	Common with paroxetine
Dry mouth	Appears less frequently than with the TCAs	Tremor	Common with paroxetine & fluvoxamine
		Sexual	**Characteristics**
Constipation		Impotence	Common with paroxetine
Blurred vision		Decreased libido, anorgasmia and delayed ejaculation	Common side-effect of all SSRIs

The properties of the individual SSRIs are illustrated in the following tables:

C)   **The SSRI**

Table 13.10   SSRI - Fluoxetine

How supplied	Cap. 10mg, Cap. 20mg	Daily dose	Start 20 daily in the morning, increase within 2 weeks by 20mg to a max. of 80 mg/day
Action	1. Inhibiting re-uptake of Serotonin in the CNS at the pre-synaptic neurons	Precautions	1. High risk of suicide 2. Impaired kidney, liver 3. Alcohol use 4. Secreted in milk 5. May activate Mania 6. History of seizure 7. May alter glucose metabolism
Indication	1. Depression 2. OCD 3.Panic disorder	Contraindication	1 Previous use of MAOI within 14 days. 2. Hypersensitivity to the drug 3. Liver/kidney disease
Absorption	1. Rapidly absorbed in the GI tract. 2. Plasma peak 3 H.	Metabolism	1. Liver. 2. Has active metabolites Norfluoxetine
Excretion	Urine	Half-life	2 – 3 days. Metabolite 7-9 days
Tips for use	1. Take drug in morning 2. Avoid alcohol 3. Avoid hazardous activities		

Side-Effect	Frequency		Stop the drug immediately
	Common	**Rare**	
Constipation	√		
Dyspepsia	√		
Vomiting	√		
Dry mouth	√		
Increased appetite	√		
Dizziness	√		
Agitation	√		
Hypotension	√		
Impaired sleep	√		
Headache	√		
Weight Loss	√		
Impotence		√	
Fatigue		√	
Decreased Libido	√		
Amenorrhea		√	

Table 13.11   SSRI – Citalopram

How supplied	Tab. 20mg Tab 40 mg	Daily dose	Start 20mg a day, increase within 1 week to a max. of 40 mg/day
Action	1. Inhibiting re-uptake of Serotonine in the CNS at the pre-synaptic neurons	**Precautions**	1. Urine retention 2. Impaired kidney, liver 3. Convulsions 4. Alcohol use 5. Secreted in milk 6. May activate Mania
Indication	1. Depression 2. OCD 3. Panic disorder	**Contraindication**	1 Previous use of MAOI within 14 days. 2. Hypersensitivity to the drug
Absorption	1. Rapidly absorbed in the GI tract. 2. Plasma peak 4. H.	**Metabolism**	1. Liver. By cytocrome P- 450 3A4 and P – 450 2C19. Has inactive metabolites
Excretion	Urine 20%	**Half-life**	35 h.
Tips for use	1. Take drug regardless of meals 2. Can be taken morning or evening 3. Avoid alcohol 4. Recommend use of high fibre diet for constipation 5. Avoid hazardous activities		

Side-Effect	**Frequency**		Stop the drug immediately
	Common	**Rare**	
Constipation	√		
Flatulence	√		
Vomiting	√		

Dry mouth	√		
Ano-rexia/ ab-dominal cramps	√		
Dizzi-ness	√		
Agitation	√		√
Hypoten-sion	√		
Anxiety	√		√
Migraine	√		
Weight gain	√		
Delayed Ejacula-tion		√	
Suicide risk		√	√
De-creased Libido	√		
Amenor-rhea		√	

Table 13.12   SSRI – Sertraline (Zoloft)

How supplied	Tab. 50mg Tab 100 mg	Daily dose	Start 50mg a day, increase within 1 week to a max. of 200 mg/day
Action	1. Inhibiting re-up-take of Serotonine in the CNS at the pre-synaptic neurons	Precautions	1. Impaired kidney, liver 2. Alcohol use 3. Secreted in milk 4. May activate Mania
Indica-tion	1. Depression 2. OCD 3. Panic disorder	Contraindi-cation	1 Previous use of MAOI within 14 days. 2. Hypersensitivity to the drug
Absorp-tion	1. Absorbed in the GI tract. Increase with food 2. Plasma peak six to eight hours	Metabolism	1. Liver. Has active metabolite n-desmeth-ylsertraline
Excre-tion	1. Urine 2. Faeces	Half-life	26 h.
Tips for use	1. Take drug with food 2. Can be taken morning or evening once daily 3. Avoid alcohol 4. Recommend use of high fibre diet for constipation 5. Avoid hazardous activities		

Side-Effect	Frequency		Stop the drug immediately
	Common	Rare	
Constipa-tion	√		
Flatu-lence	√		
Vomiting	√		

Dry mouth	√		
Ano-rexia/ abdominal cramps	√		
Dizziness	√		
Agitation	√		
Palpita-tion	√		
Anxiety	√		
Headache	√		
Weight loss	√		
Delayed Ejacula-tion		√	
Suicide risk		√	√
De-creased Libido	√		
Hot flushes		√	

Table 13.13   SSRI – Paroxetine (Aropax,Paxil)

How supplied	Tab. 10mg Tab 20 mg	Daily dose	Start 20mg a day, increase within 1 week to a max. of 50 mg/ day
Action	1. Inhibiting re-uptake of Serotonine in the CNS at the pre-synaptic neurons	Precautions	1. Impaired kidney, liver 2. Alcohol use 3. Secreted in milk 4. May activate Mania 5. May cause hyponatremia
Indication	1. Depression 2. OCD 3. Panic disorder	Contraindication	1 Previous use of MAOI within 14 days. 2. Hypersensitivity to the drug
Absorption	1. Absorbed in the GI tract. Increase with food 2. Plasma peak six to eight hours	Metabolism	1. Liver. Conjugated metabolites quickly cleared
Excretion	1. Urine	Half-life	
Tips for use	1. Take drug in the morning 2. Monitor blood Na in elderly 3. Avoid alcohol 4. Recommend use of high fibre diet for constipation 5. Avoid hazardous activities		

Side-Effect	Frequency		Stop the drug immediately
	Common	Rare	
Constipation	√		
Flatulence	√		

Vomiting	√		
Dry mouth	√		
Ano-rexia/ ab-dominal cramps	√		
Dizzi-ness	√		
Agitation	√		
Palpita-tion	√		
Anxiety	√		
Head-ache	√		
Weight loss	√		
Delayed Ejacula-tion		√	
Suicide risk		√	√
De-creased Libido	√		
Photo-sensitive		√	

Table 13.14   Bupropion (Wellbutrin)

How supplied	Tab. 150mg	Daily dose	Start 150 in the morning, increase within 3 days by 150mg to a max. of 450 mg/day
Action	1. Inhibiting re-up-take of Dopamine, Serotonin & no-radrenaline in the CNS at the pre-syn-aptic neurons	Precautions	1. History of epilepsy 2. Impaired kidney, liver 3. History of bulimia 4. Alcohol use 5. Secreted in milk 6. May activate Mania 7. Recent MI
Indica-tion	1. Depression 2.Smoke cessation	Contraindi-cation	1 Previous use of MAOI within 14 days. 2. Hypersensitivity to the drug 3. Epilepsy
Absorp-tion	1. Rapidly absorbed in the GI tract. 2. Plasma peak 3 H.	Metabolism	1. Liver. Induces its own metabolism. 2. Has active metabolites
Excre-tion	Urine 20%	Half-life	8 - 24 h.
Tips for use	1. Take drug in morning, last dose at 3pm 2. Minimum 6 hour interval between dosing 3. Avoid alcohol 4. Not to use zyban concomitantly 5. Avoid hazardous activities		

Side-Effect	Frequency		Stop the drug immediately
	Common	Rare	
Consti-pation	√		
Dyspep-sia	√		

Vomiting	√		
Dry mouth	√		
Increase appetite	√		
Dizziness	√		
Agitation	√		
Hypotension	√		
Impaired sleep	√		
Headache	√		
Weight gain	√		
Impotence		√	
Convulsions		√	√
Decreased Libido	√		
Amenorrhea		√	

Table 13.15   Mirtazapine (Remeron)

How supplied	Tab. 15mg Tab. 30 mg	Daily dose	Start 15mg in the evening, increase within 3 days by 15mg to a max. of 45 mg/day
Action	1. Potent antagonist of 5-HT2, 5HT3 (Serotonin)	Precautions	1. History of CVA 2. Impaired kidney, liver 3. History of Epilepsy 4. Alcohol use 5. Possibly secreted in milk 6. May activate Mania 7. Glaucoma 8. Hypotension
Indication	1. Depression	Contraindication	1 Previous use of MAOI within 14 days. 2. Hypersensitivity to the drug
Absorption	1. Rapidly absorbed in the GI tract. 2. Plasma peak 2 H.	Metabolism	1. Liver.
Excretion	1. Urine 2. Faeces	Half-life	20 - 40 h.
Tips for use	1. Take drug in the evening 2. Monitor agranulocitosis (rare) 3. Avoid alcohol 4. Monitor liver function 5. Avoid hazardous activities		

Side-Effect	Frequency		Stop the drug immediately
	Common	**Rare**	
Constipation	√		

Dyspepsia	√		
Vomiting	√		
Dry mouth	√		
Increased appetite	√		
Dizziness	√		
Agitation	√		
Hypotension	√		
Somnolence	√		
Abnormal dreams	√		
Headache	√		
Weight gain	√		
Impotence		√	
Convulsions		√	√
Decreased Libido	√		
Agranulocytosis		√	√

Table 13.16   SNRI – Venlafaxine (Efexor)

How supplied	Cap. 75mg, Cap. 150mg	Daily dose	Start 75mg daily in the morning, increase within 1 week by 75mg to a max. of 225mg/day
Action	1. Inhibiting re-uptake of Serotonin & Noradrenaline in the CNS at the pre-synaptic neurons	**Precautions**	1. High Blood Pressure 2. Impaired kidney, liver 3. Alcohol use 4. Secreted in milk 5. May activate Mania 6. History of seizure
Indication	1. Depression 2. GAD 3.Panic disorder	**Contraindication**	1 Previous use of MAOI within 14 days. 2. Hypersensitivity to the drug 3. Liver/kidney disease
Absorption	1. Rapidly absorbed in the GI tract	**Metabolism**	2. Liver. 3. Has active metabolites ODV
Excretion	Urine	**Half-life**	5 H.
Tips for use	1. Take drug in morning 2. Avoid alcohol 3. Avoid hazardous activities 4. Hypertensive patients must monitor blood pressure regularly		
Side-Effect	**Frequency** **Common**	**Rare**	Stop the drug immediately

Constipation	√		Hepatitis
Flatulence	√		Jaundice
Vomiting	√		Anaphylactic reaction
Dry mouth	√		Urticaria
Anorexia	√		Glaucoma
Dizziness	√		
Agitation	√		
Hypertension		√	
Impaired sleep	√		
Headache	√		
Weight Loss	√		
Impotence		√	
Fatigue		√	
Decreased Libido	√		
Abnormal ejaculation		√	

Table 13.17   SNRI – Duloxetine (Cymbalta)

How supplied	Cap. 30mg, Cap. 60mg	Daily dose	Start 30mg daily in the morning, increase within 1 week to 60mg. in resistant cases, increase up to a max. dose of 120mg/day
Action	1. Inhibiting re-uptake of Serotonin & Noradrenaline in the CNS at the pre-synaptic neurons	**Precautions**	1. Impaired kidney, liver 2. Alcohol use 3. Secreted in milk 4. May activate Mania 5. History of seizure
Indication	1. Depression 2.Generalised anxiety disorder (GAD) 3.Panic disorder 4.Neuropathic pain 5.Fibromyalgia 6.Stress urinary incontinence 7. Chronic fatigue syndrome	**Contraindication**	1 Previous use of MAOI within 14 days. 2. Hypersensitivity to the drug 3. Liver/kidney disease 4. Co-administration with thioridazine should be avoided
Absorption	1.Rapidly absorbed in the GI tract. Peak plasma concentration 6 h.	**Metabolism**	1. Liver. 2. Has several metabolites 3. Metabolised by CYP 450, 2D6 isozymes
Excretion	1 Urine 70% 2. Faeces 20%	**Half-life**	12.5 H. Steady state achieved in 3 days
Tips for use	1. Take drug in morning 2. Avoid alcohol 3. Avoid hazardous activities 4. No effect on blood pressure 5 Food delays the time to reach peak plasma from 6 to 10 H.		

Side-Effect	Frequency		Stop the drug immediately
	Common	**Rare**	
Consti-pation	√		Hepatitis
Head-ache	√		Jaundice
Nausea	√		Anaphylactic reaction
Dry mouth	√		Urticaria
Somno-lence	√		Glaucoma
Sweat-ing	√		
Insom-nia	√		
Fatigue	√		
Weight loss	√		
De-creased libido	√		
Ab-normal ejacula-tion		√	

The pharmacological treatment of depression requires highly specialised expertise. The purpose of this brief overview is to provide basic information regarding the antidepressants and their use. However, the information provided should never be substituted for a proper professional evaluation and adequate treatment which should be given only by a certified expert in that field.

Key Points

- Antidepressants are highly effective in the treatment of depression.
- SSRIs are the first line of treatment due to their effectiveness, reduced side-effects and high compliance rates.
- All antidepressants exert their Pharmacological effect on the Brain monoamines: Serotonin, Noradrenaline and Dopamine.
- All antidepressants have one to three weeks' delayed clinical response.
- Early treatment termination is accompanied by high relapse rates.
- Sudden treatment termination can result in discontinuation syndrome.

References

1. Dawson, R. (1998). Maintenance strategies for unipolar depression: an observational study of levels of treatment and recurrence. *Journal of Affective Disorders*, 49: 31 – 44.
2. NICE. (2004). Depression: Management of depression in primary and secondary care. *National Clinical Practice Guideline* Number 23. London: National Institute for Clinical Excellence.
3. Pampallona, S. (2004). Combined pharmacotherapy and psychological treatment for depression. *Archives of General Psychiatry*, 61: 714 – 719.
4. Wallis, C. (2005). The new science of happiness. *Time*, 165 (3), January 17, 2005, A2 – A9:

Suggested Reading

1.   *Professional's Handbook of Psychotropic Drugs.* (2001). Pennsylvania: Sprinhouse.
2.   *Principals and Practice of Psychopharmacotherapy.* (2006). (4th ed.). Lippincott: Williams & Wilkins.
3.   Arana, G., Rosenbaum, J.F. *Handbook of Psychiatric Drug Therapy.* (2000). (4th ed.). Lippincott: Williams & Wilkins.
4.   Stein, G. & Wilkinson, G. (eds). (2007). *Seminars in General Adult Psychiatry.* (2nd ed.).The Royal College of Psychiatrists.
5.   Stern, T., Rosenbaum, J., Fava, M., Biderman, J., Rauch, S. (2008). *Massachusetts General Hospital Comprehensive Clinical Psychiatry.* Mosby Elsevier inc.

FOURTEEN

The Use of CBT in Divorce

"Nothing in life is to be feared. It is only to be understood".
Marie Curie

The Purpose

The purpose of this chapter is to explain **what CBT is** and how it **should** be used in **coping with** the divorce emotional conditions.

Introduction to the Basic Cognitive Therapy Principals

Cognitive Behavioural Therapy or CBT for short is a specific psychological treatment modality, originated and developed by A. T. Beck for the treatment of anxiety and depression.

Over the years, CBT treatment was extended to treat other emotional conditions such as Obsessive Compulsive Disorder (OCD), Post Traumatic Stress Disorder (PTSD), Bipolar mood disorder and Schizophrenia.

The basic concept of CBT for anxiety and depression maintains that the negative emotional state develops pursuant to a distorted, negative cognitive process. In other words, your feelings are the result of the way you think. If you have positive thoughts you will feel good, while if you continue having negative thoughts you will inevitably feel depressed and anxious.

The way you think and see the world is based on your value system which is established early in life. If, from childhood, you learn to view your surroundings as bad and hostile while viewing yourself as unworthy, then it is not surprising that later in life you will be prone to developing low self-esteem and other negative emotional states. According to CBT theory, your thought process requires three principal components:

- Core beliefs
- Basic assumption filter
- Negative automatic thoughts (NAT)

The Core Belief System

The core belief system is a subconscious construct which contains the basic beliefs you hold about yourself, about the world and about other people. Your initial belief system develops early during the period of complete dependency and limited reasoning capabilities. As a result of such a constellation, your initial value system is a mirror copy of your parents' views as well as those of all the other significant figures in your life. Over time, your basic core beliefs become slowly modified by your life experiences, and by the interactions with other figures you meet. As an adult, your personal views and core beliefs are firmly established and make you think the way you do.

Childhood exposure to negative events and to negative feedback does little to build positive self-esteem and a positive realistic value system. In addition, being exposed to negative life experiences will further enhance negative core beliefs, and will badly damage your fragile self-esteem. Traumatic interactions with others, such as being bullied at school, or being mentally or physically abused by your parents can further negatively affect the way you see and interact with others. Growing up with mental or physical deprivation will also badly affect the way you look at the world.

Your personal core belief system is mostly unconscious and so you are not really able to access it. Your basic values shape the type of thoughts that you eventually become 'aware' of.

Remember, the thoughts you hold are only a reflection of your opinions, and do not represent real, hard facts therefore your thoughts are amenable to change. If you can be made aware of the negative quality of your thoughts then you can, with hard work, modify and change your thoughts to positive ones. The end result of such thought transformation will eventually change your negative emotional tone into a positive emotional response.

Examples of negative core beliefs are:
- "I must be perfect, otherwise I am a loser".
- "I must depend on others to survive".
- "I must please others to be accepted".
- "I am not clever enough therefore I will never be able to be a ...".
- "My happiness depends on others".
- "It's my fault".
- "I'm boring".
- "I'm a failure".
- "I can't trust anyone".
- "I'm bad".

Having such a negative view about yourself or the world will invariably result in negative self-esteem and unhappy, negative emotional reactions.

You can try to identify the pattern with which you see yourself, others and life in general. Looking at your core belief is an ambitious journey into your value system that controls the way you see yourself, which ultimately influences the way you interact with others. As the main component of your core belief system are the basic premises you hold about yourself, others and the world. Completing Table 14.1 will help you to unlock your basic core beliefs.

Table 14.1   Unlocking your core beliefs:

The way you see yourself	Attributes
I am:	I am:
I am:	I am:
I am:	I am:
The way you see others	**Attributes**
The way I see my family is:	
The way I see my co-workers:	
The way I see my friends:	
The way I see my neighbours:	
The way you see the world	**Attributes**
The place I work is:	
My neighbourhood is:	

The Basic Assumption Filter

In addition to the basic core belief system, the cognitive process involves a filter mechanism which serves the function of painting every incoming thought with either a positive or a negative colour. The cognitive filter consists of the assumptions you hold regarding life.

A dysfunctional assumption filter is a rigid and over-generalised system which often involves conditional statements such as, "If I want to do X then I should do that", or "I must do Y in order to be ...". Frequent use of conditional statements will further enhance the creation of negative automatic thoughts.

The Negative Automatic Thoughts (NAT)

Negative automatic thoughts are the conscious thoughts which automatically surface in response to life events. In other words, the negative automatic thought is the first thought that will pop into your head in response to anything that happens in your life.

The negative automatic thoughts are distorted, conscious interpretations of external events. The normal thoughts you have can either be positive, neutral or negative. The emotional tone you assign to each thought can be metaphorically viewed as the colour with which you paint each thought.

Having a mostly basic negative core belief system coupled with a mainly dysfunctional assumption filter will generate mostly negative interpretations of reality in the form of negative automatic thoughts. Having abundant negative life events can activate an excessive use of the negative component of the thought process, while having positive life experiences can activate the positive component of the cognitive processes.

The most common used automatic negative thoughts are illustrated in Table 14.2.

Table 14.2   The Most Common Negative Automatic Thoughts

NAT	Definition	Example
Over-generali-sation	Using a single fact to draw a wrong conclusion	When you think 'always', 'never', 'everyone'.
Magnifying	Blowing things out of proportion	Making mountains out of small hills.
Black or white approach	No alternatives or other options available	Nothing is good.
Jumping to conclusions	Making decisions without having all the facts	So he said that he won't be able to come. Well of course he doesn't want to come because …
Catastrophising	The worst outcome is exaggerated	I will never have enough money to pay my bills.
Rejecting the positive	Ignoring the positive aspects of the situation	The money he deposited in my account is probably a once-off event and will never happen again.
Blaming	Looking for someone to be responsible for the situation. More commonly, self-blame	It's my fault...
Mind-reading	Knowing what others think	When you assume things that are never said or done
Labelling	Everything is labelled negatively	I am useless, I am a failure. My lawyer is useless...
'Should' statement	Place demands on yourself	I should go to... I must do that...

Negative automatic thoughts are, in essence, a cognitive dissonance. They are a biased interpretation of life circumstances. NATs are maladaptive, as they foster negative emotional reactions and result in dysfunctional behaviour, low self-esteem, anxiety and depression. Having excessive use of negative automatic thoughts as a principal cognitive mode is a highly unproductive and an undesirable cognitive process, as it results in an automatic negative interpretation of life which can lead to anxiety and depression.

The complex interaction between those three CBT domains is illustrated in Figure 14.3, while Figure 14.4 describes the cognitive process according to the CBT model.

Figure 14.3   The Cognitive Process According to the CBT Model

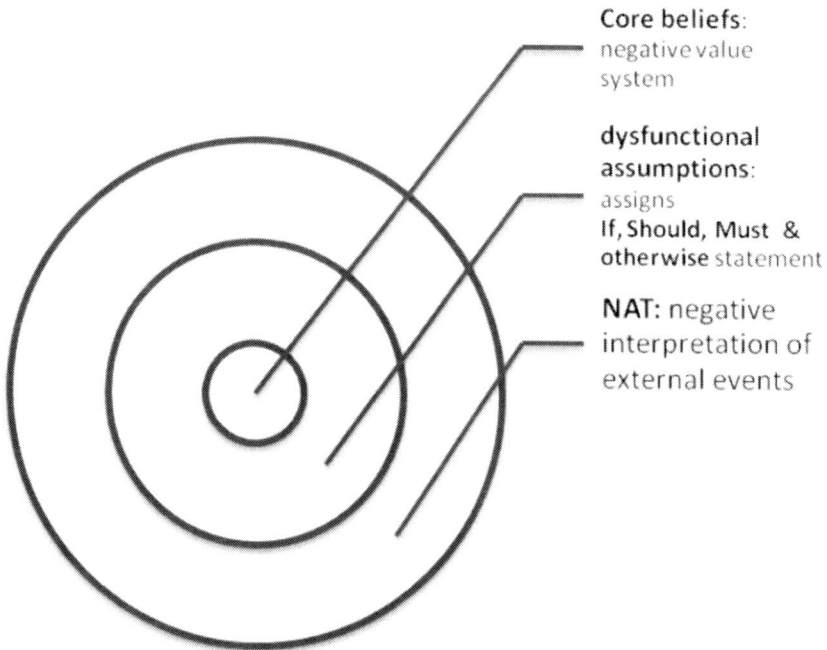

Core beliefs: negative value system

dysfunctional assumptions: assigns If, Should, Must & otherwise statement

NAT: negative interpretation of external events

Figure 14.4   Example of the Cognitive Process of the CBT Model

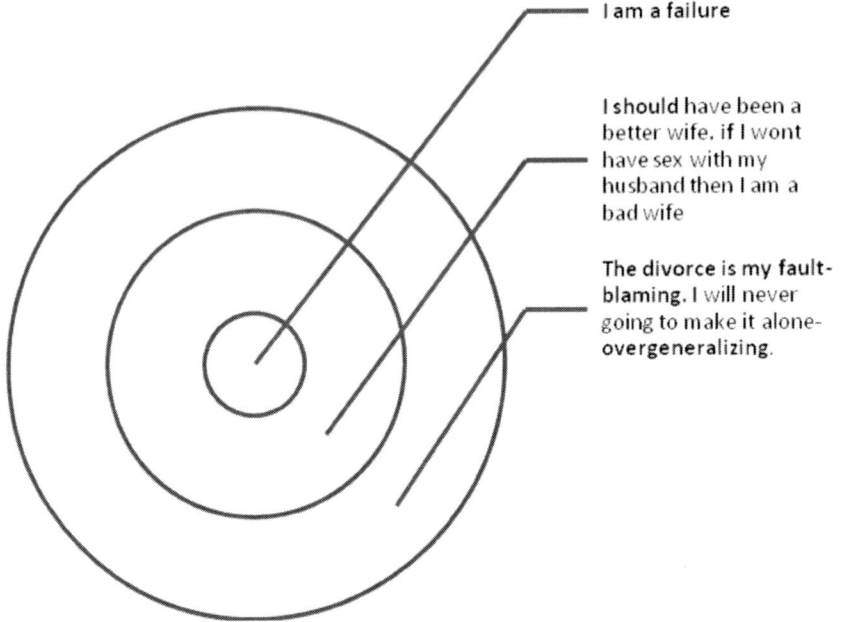

I am a failure

I should have been a better wife. if I wont have sex with my husband then I am a bad wife

The divorce is my fault-blaming. I will never going to make it alone-overgeneralizing.

In depression, there is an excessive and almost exclusive use of NATs regardless of the nature of the situation. Similarly, during the divorce, it is highly common to see an excessive use of NATs due to high stress and multiple conflicts. As the only accessible component of the thought process is the NATs, it is the focus and the prime target of the CBT model. Changing your NATs to a more realistic alternative will positively influence your mood. Access to the NATs requires careful attention to their existence and regular practice.

Figure 14.5 illustrates an example of how such negative automatic thoughts develop as the result of divorce-related events, and how they can influence mood and behaviour:

Figure 14.5   Example of the Divorce Effects and the Distorted NAT on Emotions and Behaviour.

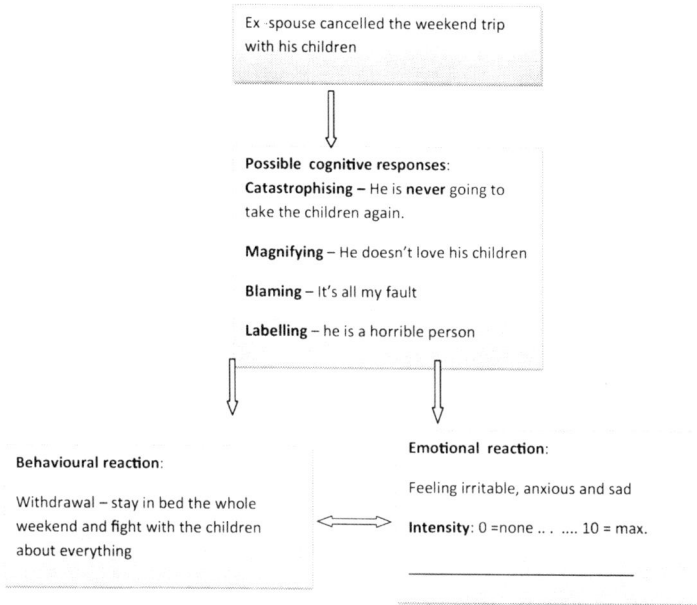

In this example scenario, instead of validating the actual reasons that led to the cancellation of the weekend trip, you rather automatically resort to several negative automatic thoughts that make you sad, irritable and withdrawn.

Mood and behaviour are strongly influenced by life events and by the way these are interpreted. Negative interpretations of whatever is going on in your life will make you feel depressed, while positive interpretations will help you to feel and cope better with your life. Changing your negative views about life circumstances to a more optimistic attitude will improve your responses, and will reduce your stress. As most of the cognitive components are unconscious, with the exception of the automatic negative thoughts, addressing and changing their negative nature into a more optimistic format will have a dramatic effect on mood and behaviour.

The aim of the CBT is to help you identify your conscious negative automatic thoughts, challenge their validity, and then formulate a different and more realistic alternative. The new alternative thought will be without the cognitive bias of the previous automatic thought.

Studies on depressed patients using CBT techniques showed a significant reduction in the depressive symptoms and behavioural improvement.

The negative automatic thought finder is a simple tool that will help you identify and challenge their validity and consequently improve your mood and your goal-directed actions.

Negative Automatic Thought Finder:

Table 14.6 contains several examples of classical divorce-related events with some common related NATs as well as suggested alternative interpretations.

Table 14.6   Example of Common Divorce-Related Events with Possible Corresponding NATs and Functional Alternative Thoughts

The event	The thought	Alternative interpretation
Your ex-spouse requested a reduction in his/her maintenance payments.	**A Must statement-** *I **must** punish him/her.*	*I will discuss how to deal with my ex-spouse's requests with my lawyer.*
Received the divorce summons from the sheriff.	**Labelling -** *I couldn't maintain my marriage which means I am a complete failure.*	*Getting a divorce opens up new possibilities to meet interesting people.*

Received the divorce summons.	**Blaming** - *It is **my fault** that s/he left me.*	*We divorced because we were not compatible.*
Stayed alone over the weekend.	**All or Nothing** - *I will never get married again.*	*I don't want to get involved again right now, but in the future I will be open to new adventures.*
Stayed alone at home over the week-end.	**Jumping to conclusions** *I can't live alone.*	*It is time to start my new free life alone.*
Attending a divorce help group meeting.	**Over-Generalisation- Everyone** *is getting divorced lately.*	*Some people get divorced, others stay married.*
Looking at your empty bank statement.	**Jumping to conclusions-** *I will never be able to maintain myself.*	*I will start looking for work. Finally I can be economically independent.*

As you can see, a single event can generate several negative automatic thoughts. The purpose of this exercise is to train yourself to see how quickly you assume the worst possible explanation for any given event.

Initially it will be very difficult to identify the distorted cognitive pattern with which you see the world. However, with some exercise, you can train yourself to become an expert negative thought finder, and by forcing yourself to make a more optimistic alternative explanation you will notice how your overall mood changes.

When you complete Table 14.7 you need to concentrate hard to remember the first thought that came into your mind when you encountered a specific event. Remember, the thought you had was your thought. In addition, there is not only one alternative explanation for any given event. You can try to formulate as many alternative interpretations for any given incident you had during the day and think of how you can validate them.

Start completing Table 14.7 by identifying a specific event related to your divorce. Then try to remember what your initial thought was in response to the incident as well as how you felt and behaved. If your mind goes blank and you are unable to remember any automatic thoughts, then describe the incident and start to describe how you felt about it and what you did. Starting by describing your emotions might help you to re-live the event and bring your NATs back to life.

Table 14.7   Identify Your NATs and Their Impact on Your Mood and Behaviour

Divorce event: _____
_____
_____

⇩

See if you have any of those automatic thoughts:

Catastrophising : No / Yes: what _____

Magnifying: No / Yes, what _____

Blaming: No / Yes, What _____

Labelling: No / Yes, What _____

Mind-reading: No / Yes, What _____

Jumping to conclusions: No / Yes, What _____

Rejecting the positive: No / Yes, What _____

⇩   ⇩

Your behavioural reaction: _____   ⇐⇒   Your emotional reaction:

_____   I am feeling:_____

_____

_____   _____

_____   Intensity: 0=none...10= max.: _____

After several practice runs you will be able to see the extent to which you use NATs in response to your divorce circumstances. Once you feel comfortable with your abilities to identify the NATs you use, then try to create an alternative interpretation of the event and observe how it can change your emotions and your behaviour.

You can capture your daily events, your NATs and your emotional state in Table 14.8.

Remember, you can change the way you see yourself, life and others, and consequently, you will change the way you feel.

Table 14.8   Daily Activity and NAT Modifier

Day/ time	Event	Your negative thought	Your emotional reaction Intensity: 0 = none 10= max	Alternative thought	
				Emotional reaction	**Intensity score**
Sun. 11 am	*Example: the priest ignored me*	*It's because I am divorced* – **Jumping to conclusions**	*depressed* *10*	*The church was full. Maybe he did not see me* *Relieved, happy*	*10*
Mon.					

Tue.					
Wed.					
Thu.					
Fri.					
Sat.					

The ability to identify and change your core beliefs and your negative automatic thoughts will be an important step on the road to reducing your stress and improving your emotions.

Key Points

- CBT is an effective psychological treatment for emotional disorders.
- Negative automatic thoughts are conscious negative interpretations of life circumstances.
- Negative automatic thoughts can lead to anxiety and depression.
- Negative automatic thoughts are conscious and accessible, and can be modified.
- Changing your negative thoughts to positive alternatives will improve your emotional state.

Suggested reading

39. Wright, J.H. (2006). *Learning Cognitive Behaviour Therapy.* American Psychiatric Publishing, inc.
40. Persons, J.B. (1989). *Cognitive Therapy in Practice.* W.W. Norton & company, Inc.
41. Edelmam, S. (2007). *Change your Thinking.* Marlowe & Company.
42. Branch, R. & Willson, R. (2007). *Cognitive Behavioural Therapy workbook for dummies.* John Wiley & Sons, Ltd.

FIFTEEN

Anger in Divorce

"Anyone can become angry. That is easy. But to be angry with the right person, to the right degree, at the right time, for the right purpose and the right way, that is not easy".
Aristotle

The Purpose

The purpose of this chapter is to explain anger, and its treatment.

Introduction

Anger is a normal, universal human emotional state which usually develops as a reaction to external provocation. However, anger can also develop pursuant to an internal, intra-psychic event. Anger can be expressed either externally or internally. External expressions of anger manifest through verbal and behavioural gestures towards the one who provoked it. Self-directed anger manifests in behaviour directed towards oneself, as a reaction to perceiving personal mistakes or personal shortcomings.

Divorce interpersonal conflicts are the perfect arena in which anger can develop and be externally discharged at the ex-spouse and his/her legal team, or directed towards the family and friends. In some divorces, anger becomes the most prominent emotional state which dominates the interaction, and invariably damages any possible positive divorce outcome. Too much and uncontrolled anger will sever the relationship with your ex-spouse, as well as damaging your self-esteem, and can lead to unwanted legal consequences.

Anger can develop at any stage during the divorce process with various degrees of intensity, ranging from a mild behavioural manifestation expressed with sarcasm and irritability to a complete lack of control resulting in physical assault and damage to property.

Anger has a wide range of emotional, behavioural and verbal forms that often manifest in an interpersonal context.

The emotional forms of anger
- Feeling bitter
- Feeling angry, cross
- Feeling at boiling point
- Feeling frustrated

The verbal forms of anger
- Verbal procrastination
- Verbal rage attacks
- Screaming
- Cursing

The behavioural forms of anger
- Vindictive behaviour
- Breaking household furniture
- Minor physical assault: pushing, slapping, smacking

- Hitting
- Murder

The most common and easiest way to express your anger is by using your children as a weapon against your ex-spouse. In such a scenario, whenever you get hurt, frustrated or angry, all you need to do is to keep your children out of your ex-spouse's sight. This requires good imagination to create a convincing story to make your children unavailable to your ex-spouse. However, resorting to such strategies is always harmful to your children, and can act as a double-edged sword, as your ex-spouse may behave in the same way by showing no interest in his/her children, withholding maintenance payments or turning the children against you.

In general, anger is highly dysfunctional, destructive and is an unproductive way of coping with personal and interpersonal frustrations. Too often, the result of inappropriate discharges of anger is more conflict and further alienation.

The multiple losses experienced in divorce represent the most common catalyst that leads to frustration and anger. This anger develops as the result of the multiple losses which include the following:

- *Financial losses*: losing your home, car and many other commodities
- *Emotional losses*: losing your children, friends, previous lifestyle

Although feeling angry is quite normal in the divorce context, it is still important that you are able to express your anger in a mature, adaptive and functional manner, especially if you are interested in having a reasonable and positive future relationship with your ex-spouse.

To be angry is human. During the prehistoric era, our early human ancestors had to assert their position in the social hierarchy by showing their strength through a controlled display of angry gestures. However, in modern days, displays of anger have a very limited societal role in order to show power.

Today, any form of anger is deemed to be unacceptable and is considered to be socially maladaptive. From a very young age, one is taught to suppress anger. You have to learn quickly that the first sign of anger is undesirable, unacceptable and is a punishable offence.

The aim of such rigorous anti-anger education is to suppress your basic primordial anger instincts and to transform these to the extent that they become more socially acceptable.

A common example of socially accepted anger is a driver who exerts self-control when he is dangerously and recklessly overtaken by another driver, and only mutters to himself some "impolite" words, while a dysfunctional expression of anger in this particular scenario would be the driver who either verbally attacks the other reckless driver or tries to assault him physically, which is common road-rage behaviour.

What are the Principal Characteristics of Anger?

According to Zillmann, 1998, anger has several characteristics which include the following:

1. *A Goal:* Anger always has a goal. The goal of anger is to eliminate the source that originally provoked your anger.
2. *Means:* Anger always has a means. The means by which anger is able to be discharged is the action you take to get rid of the source of your anger.
3. *Direction:* Anger always has a direction. The direction of anger is always aimed *against the source that provoked your anger*. When the source is internal, then anger will be self-directed leading to cutting and other suicidal gestures.
4. *Physiological state:* Anger is associated with *a state of physiological arousal* which prepares your body for action. The greater the anger

you feel, the stronger the physiological reaction will be.

5. ***Behavioural expression***: Anger is expressed by your *hostile behavioural action*.

6. ***The situation:*** Anger *develops in conflict and provocative situations.* Anger has a tendency to *escalate as the situation remains provocative*. Mild provocation induces a mild reaction while increased provocation culminates in an aggressive outburst.

7. ***The baseline emotional state***: Anger creates a *high excitatory physiological tone* which can fuel a minor conflict into a disproportionate fight, for example, a divorced woman with financial difficulties will be highly upset and might react with a sudden and disproportionate rage when she learns that her ex-spouse's monthly maintenance payment has been stopped.

8. ***Distorted cognitive appraisal:*** During the anger state there is a *specific distorted cognitive state of mind which facilitates inappropriate behaviour*. In a normal situation, the primary objectives of proper cognitive functions are to avoid self-harm. Such objectives are accomplished by regular monitoring of the situation, evaluating the possible reactions to any external insult, as well as examining the possible consequences of your reaction. High levels of anger create a cognitive distortion state which leads to inappropriate appraisal of the situation and, consequently, to inappropriate reactions. In addition, during an anger state there is a heightened emotional arousal which causes a temporary shutdown of your logical thinking, thus leading to a narrowed response range and ignoring the broader consequences and the possible implications of your actions.

9. ***Low empathic state:*** *Anger reduces your empathic abilities.* Normally, most people are empathic and sensitive to others' needs. The empathic ability is unique to the human race, and is an emotional reaction which enables each person to place himself in

another's shoes. In other words, empathy allows you to feel and to see what another person experiences in a given situation. The empathic capability varies among people and is reduced or non-existent during severe anger states.

10.   ***Poor logical reasoning:*** *Anger reduces your logical reasoning.* An angry person acts before he thinks. The attitude of "I don't care what will happen to me or to the other person" prevails. Anger reduces the logical reasoning regarding the possible consequences of one's actions.

In addition to the anger inherent cognitive distortion, any additional factor that will further impair your cognitive functions will worsen the potential for an anger outburst.

The most common examples of anger enhancers are alcohol, or any other mind-altering drugs such as amphetamines, LSD, Cocaine or Heroin. Those drugs strongly affect cognition and judgment. Excess alcohol use causes impaired social judgment and reduces inhibitions. People under the influence of alcohol tend to misjudge the situation and act before they think. In addition, the use of mind-altering substances lowers your frustration tolerance and increases your propensity to aggressive outbursts.

The Biological Basis of Anger

During anger there is a hyper activity state of the *amygdala*, the *hippocampus* and the hypothalamus with increased levels of Noradrenaline and Cortisol.

Anger usually develops in the context of a conflict situation which generates high levels of frustration. In other words, you become angry when others irritate or frustrate you.

Studies show that the natural expression of anger can be modified by cultural influences. Exposure to violence at an early age by watching violent movies on TV or playing violent computer games, or by witnessing or directly experiencing physical abuse can increase the likelihood of aggressive behaviour during adulthood. Similarly, it was shown that the availability of weapons is associated with a higher likelihood of violent behaviour. Therefore, although anger should be viewed as a normal response to an interpersonal conflict, when it becomes inappropriate or excessive it becomes socially unacceptable and unproductive as the inability to control anger might have unpleasant social and legal implications.

From the biological point of view there are two types of aggressive behaviour:

1. *The Predatory type of aggression* – predatory aggression is a behaviour used during hunting.
2. *The Defensive type of aggression*: defensive aggression is a behaviour used to avoid a fight and helps to prepare the individual to flee from the adverse situation.

Both types of aggression have a similar biological substrate. Studies on laboratory animals showed that the stimulation of the *lateral part* of the *hypothalamus* elicits a predatory type of aggression, while the stimulation of *the medial part* of the *hypothalamus* elicits a defensive type of aggression. Animal studies conducted by E. S. Higgins in 2007 on cats showed that the biological aim of the defensive aggression is to warn and frighten the adversary with a specific behaviour that includes hissing, arching the back, paw swiping and pilo-erection.

The complex physiological basis of anger is illustrated in Figure 15.1.

Table 15.1   The Physiology of Anger

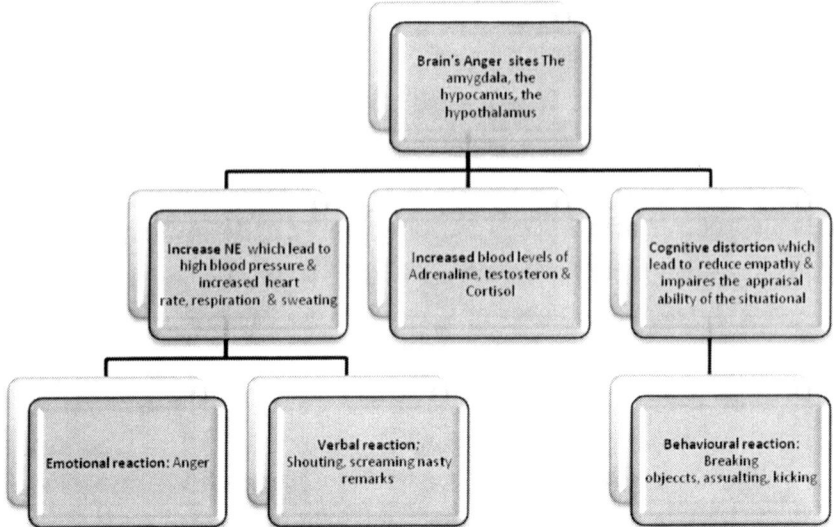

What are the Neurotransmitters and Hormones that Mediate Aggression?

Anger involves the following hormones and neurotransmitters:

1. **Testosterone** – testosterone is the principal male hormone and is widely believed to be associated with aggressive behaviour. However, the scientific literature presents conflicting evidence regarding testosterone's direct link with aggression. A study which proves such a connection was conducted by E. S. Higgins in 2007 on male prisoners, and was able to show a connection between high testosterone levels and aggression. In this study, the socially dominant prisoners had higher plasma testosterone levels than the more submissive and less aggressive prisoners.

    However, another study conducted by the same authors on sexual predators treated with anti-testosterone medications (antiandrogens) had contrary results. This study showed that although the subjects treated with antiadrogens exhibited a significant decrease in their active sexual behaviour, they showed very little change in their aggressive behaviour.

2. **Vasopressin** – vasopressin which is also known as the antidiuretic hormone plays an important role in the body's water balance causing water retention. However, recent studies by E. Higgins showed that the blockade of vasopressin receptors can decrease aggressive behaviour.

3. **Serotonin** - serotonin is a neurotransmitter involved in mood regulation. Studies conducted by Higgins on monkeys showed that monkeys with higher rates of violence and aggression had lower levels of the serotonine metabolite 5-HIAA in their cerebro-spinal fluid (CSF). This study demonstrated that the monkeys with the lower serotonin metabolite were more likely to engage in rough interactions that escalated into unrestrained aggression with a higher probability of injury. Another similar study conducted by Higgins on monkeys found a direct correlation between low levels of 5-HIAA, which is the principal serotonin metabolite, and risk-taking behaviour. The aggressive monkeys which showed low levels of 5 –HIAA challenged the group leader despite their physical inferiority, a behaviour which placed them in danger.

   E Higgins reported that human clinical studies with SSRI (An antidepressant which modulates brain Serotonin) on aggressive schizophrenic, autistic and personality disorder patients have found that the subjects receiving SSRI medication were less aggressive in comparison with those treated with the placebo.

4. **Dopamine** - Dopamine is a neurotransmitter involved with pleasure-seeking and aggressive behaviour. The pleasure-taking activities are modulated by the dopamine levels in the *nucleus accumbens.* There are increased levels of dopamine in the *nucleus accumbens* during

activities associated with pleasure and aggression. Having sex, gambling or using cocaine also involves higher dopamine activity in the *nucleus accumbens*. Often the aggressor can experience pleasure from his behaviour which further elucidates the link between dopamine, aggression and pleasure. Another study conducted by Higgins on aggressive rats also showed higher levels of dopamine in their *nucleus accumbens* following aggressive encounters with other rats.

The Three Stages of Anger

According to D. Zillmann, 1988, anger develops in three distinctive separate stages with different behavioural manifestations. At the initial anger stage, there is a low state of physiological excitation. Judgment is minimally impaired and remains cohesive, coherent and balanced.

As the physiological overdrive increases, the ability to make an adequate appraisal of the situation substantially reduces and judgement becomes selective.

In addition, the empathic ability grossly reduces, along with increased self-concern and reduced concerns regarding the wellbeing of others. This shift towards increased self-concern coupled with poor judgement and reduced empathic attitude creates the proper cognitive platform to express aggressive behaviour. The heightened physiological arousal state combined with a higher readiness for action will make you feel eager to get into action in order to discharge the excessive energy accumulated in your muscles.

At the final anger stage, judgement becomes completely impaired. You are no longer able to monitor the situation logically. Your heightened physiological state creates a false illusion of power and feelings of invulnerability. The consequences of your actions are completely ignored or trivialised.

The behavioural progression of anger is further elaborated on in Figure 15.2.

Figure 15.2   The Behavioural Progression of Anger.

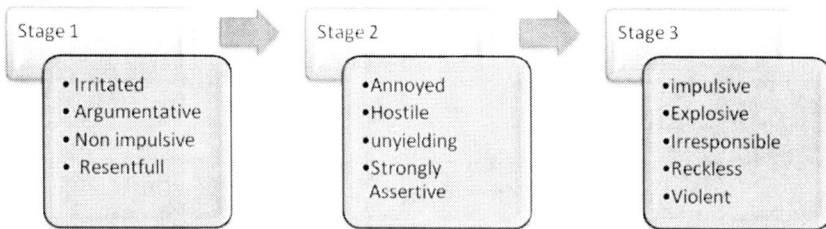

Stage 1	Stage 2	Stage 3
• Irritated • Argumentative • Non impulsive • Resentfull	•Annoyed •Hostile •unyielding •Strongly Assertive	•impulsive •Explosive •Irresponsible •Reckless •Violent

The negative aspects of anger

Anger is mostly maladaptive and socially undesirable. Anger outbursts will disrupt your interpersonal relationships and your societal ties. Having frequent anger outbursts will drain your energy, and will leave you with little time to spend on constructive activities.

Anger outbursts will lead to you to be socially isolated and will provide a negative model for your children who will consider anger as the preferred way to handle interpersonal conflicts.

Feeling constantly angry will extenuate the negative aspects of your personality. Many divorced couples often say that they hate to look in the mirror and see what a horrible person they have become.

Damage to property and frequent encounters with the law are a common and unpleasant consequence of anger outbursts. Such unacceptable behaviour can damage personal development and will ultimately jeopardise future custodial and visitation rights.

What are the Most Common Causes of Anger?

Anger develops in the context of interpersonal situations which have a high level of conflict and frustration.

The most common social causes of anger are eloquently described by R. Digiuseppe & R. C. Tafrate, 2007, in their book *"Understanding anger disorder"* and are listed in Table 15.3.

Table 15.3   The Most Common Social Causes of Anger

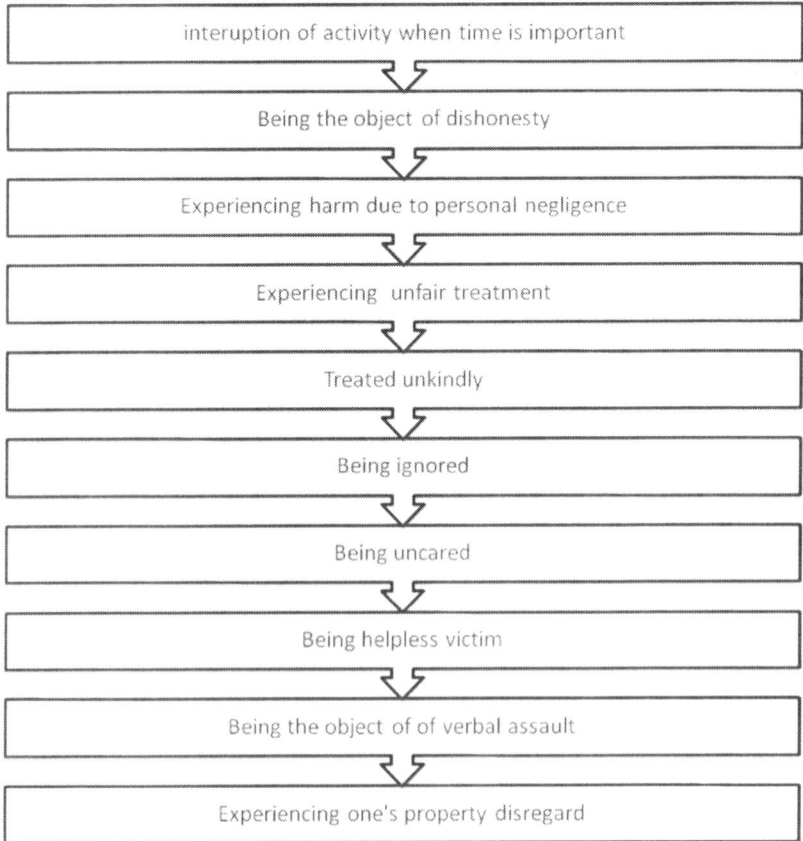

interuption of activity when time is important
Being the object of dishonesty
Experiencing harm due to personal negligence
Experiencing unfair treatment
Treated unkindly
Being ignored
Being uncared
Being helpless victim
Being the object of of verbal assault
Experiencing one's property disregard

According to Digiuseppe & Tafrate the most common precipitating social causes of anger relate either to a direct or indirect threat to one's life or to one's wellbeing. Other common social causes of anger involve suppression of one's needs or a threat to one's property. The divorce which you are going through is a fertile ground for conflict, frustration, and threatens your safety and your ability to preserve your personal needs.

In functional marriages, the loving spouses see their partner's needs as equal to their own, while in dysfunctional marriages and in couples going through divorce, they tend to place their own personal needs before those of their spouses. Such attitudes promote frustration, bitterness and anger.

The most common cause of anger during the divorce results from conflicts over financial issues and matters related to the way the children should be raised. Bruised egos and personal disappointment over the failed marriage are also a common cause of anger in divorce.

According to Averill, J., another factor which is often associated with anger relates to the perception of being unfairly treated which is a common divorce scenario.

Table 15.4 lists some common causes of divorce-related anger and their effects on you. You can add additional causes that also make you feel angry.

Table 15.4   What Makes you Angry and How Does this Affect Your Life?

What makes you angry?	How angry do you get? 0= No anger 10= Max. anger	How much control do you have over your anger? 0 = No control 10= Max. control	How greatly does anger affect your life? 0= No impact 10= Max. impact
Inter-personal issues			
You feel threatened			
You feel ignored			
Your ex-spouse treats you with disrespect			
Your ex-spouse treats your children badly			
Financial issues			
Losing financially			

You are getting an unfair deal			
Issues re-garding your chil-dren			

The Positive Aspects of Anger

Although anger is mostly maladaptive, dysfunctional and socially unacceptable, there are instances in which anger can have constructive consequences. Mild levels of anger which involve a higher physiological arousal state can motivate personal growth. During the early stages of anger your ability to focus improves substantially, and you experience an improved assertive attitude that can lead to clearer self-expression, building more visible boundaries and improving respect and better standing in other eyes.

Ventilation of Anger

Contrary to the popular assumption that venting anger is good for your health, the current psychological research data extensively disprove this notion. According to R.G. Geen (2001), anger outbursts can lead to a temporary, short-lived, limited calming effect, but more commonly, venting your anger will make you feel shame and anxiety. Similar studies conducted by Bushman, B. J. (1999), found that displayed anger provokes a retaliatory reaction that can escalate the conflict situation into a major disaster. In their study, Bushman showed that the subjects who were provoked became more aggressive when given the chance for revenge. According to Bushman, "ventilation is like using gasoline to put out fire".

In addition, unpunished aggressive behaviour tends to be reinforced. If your ex-spouse becomes accustomed to venting his/her anger freely on you or on your children without any consequences, it is more likely that such behaviour will be repeated frequently during the divorce.

How Anger Affects Your Body?

Experiencing excessive anger can lead to serious health consequences due to the presence of excessive physiological overdrive and can cause the following clinical complications:
- Hypertension
- Heart disease
- Duodenal Ulcer
- Dysfunctional immune system

Anger, Hypertension and Heart Disease

The link between anger and high blood pressure was demonstrated in many studies. Schwartz, G.E. (1981) found that angry people have a higher blood pressure compared to individuals who only experience anxiety. Such high blood pressure is thought to be the result of increased bodily Rennin and

Noradrenaline, both of which substances are directly implicated in the maintenance of the cardiovascular tone.

Hypertension is involved with the increased risk of coronary heart disease. In a clinical study conducted by Williams, J.E. (2000), 13 000 middle-aged subjects who had high scores on the anger scale were followed for five years, and were three times more likely to have suffered a heart attack. Another study conducted by Change, P.P. (2002) who followed up on 1055 male medical students over 36 years, discovered that by the age of 55, those students who were hot-tempered were five times more likely to have had a heart attack. These studies confirmed the link between hypertension, heart disease and anger.

Anger and Duodenal Ulcer

There is ample evidence to show that anger and stress may be involved in duodenal ulcers. Wolf, S. (1968) could demonstrate that angry subjects had increased secretion of hydrochloride acid in their stomachs which increased their chances of developing duodenal ulcers.

Experiencing stress also weakens the gastro intestinal defences against high levels of gastric acid resulting in injury to the lining of the gastric wall and predisposing ulcer conditions.

Anger and the Immune System

The effect of stress on the immune system was extensively investigated by Riley, V. (1981) who could demonstrate the immunosuppressive effect of stress. In his seminal study, Riley discovered that mice subjected to stress had a marked decrease in their lymphocyte count. The heightened physiological arousal diverts the body's energy resources from the immune

Dr Shlomo Brook

system to the muscles and the brain, thus increasing the vulnerability to illness.

The Common Manifestations of Anger During the Divorce

During the divorce anger can be expressed in many ways. The most commonly displayed forms of anger can be grouped into three major behavioural patterns:
*   Engaging in the displacement game
*   Engaging in the excuse game
*   Engaging in the passive aggressive game

A.   **The Displacement "Game"**

The displacement game is a common "civilized" way of expressing anger. Your angry feelings towards your ex-spouse become displaced from their primary object, which is your ex-spouse onto other subjects/people. In this scenario, you displace or re-direct your original anger towards your children, to your extended family or to your close friends and to your work colleagues. Displacing anger onto others will make them become your punching-bags and scapegoats. Your children can be blamed for anything that went wrong in the marriage and in your present situation. However, engaging in such behaviour does very little to enhance your children's self-esteem, confidence or their moods.

Feeling upset and angry with your former spouse must be dealt with in a mature way with your ex-spouse and not with anybody else. You need to address the issues that gave rise to your anger directly with your ex-spouse and leave your children or others out of your conflict zone.

B.   **The Excuse "Game"**

Another common way of expressing your anger is by using excuses. Your children become the perfect weapon with which you can express your anger towards your ex-spouse. The most common example of this "game" is to find the right excuse which will prevent your ex-spouse from seeing his/her offspring. This game is a guaranteed winner, yet it is highly counter-productive for any future relationship, and will often damage your children's ability to form a productive bond with their estranged parent.

Examples of commonly used excuses are: "The child is busy/ sick/ tired/ with a friend/ has other previous engagements, or is unable to talk to you". Despite its effectiveness, the excuse game should not be used as it sends a confusing message to your children who are not aware of your behaviour and will perceive their divorced parent as not being interested in them.

In addition, your children might discover that they are being used as a vehicle to express your anger, and might perceive your behaviour as deceptive and untrustworthy. In some cases, your children will participate voluntarily with the "excuse Game" and further alienate themselves from their parent. Both scenarios are unhealthy, and you should make an effort to avoid the use of your children as a tool to express your anger.

Completing Table 15.5 will help you to identify how much you engage in this unhealthy "excuse game".

Table 15.5   What is Your Excuse Game?

What excuse you use to hurt your ex?	How frequently you engage with it?			Are your children aware of it?	
	Rarely	Some-times	All the time	Yes	No

C.   The Passive Aggressive "Game"

Passive aggressive behaviour is another way in which you can express your anger. In this game your anger is expressed by displaying a passive attitude. Unfortunately, such an approach has limited results, although it might seem like a good idea to you to show your anger in this way as it will guarantee retaliatory anger from your ex-spouse which will further escalate the tension and will increase the conflict.

Examples of passive aggressive behaviour are missing an important joint appointment you made with your ex-spouse or with his legal advisers, or "losing" the financial agreement that your ex-spouse sent you, or "misplacing" any other important divorce document.

It is important to be able to identify and eliminate as far as possible such a passive aggressive attitude in order to minimise conflict.

The following Table, 15.6 will help you to identify your unhealthy passive aggressive behaviour.

Table 15.6   What is Your Passive Aggressive "Game"?

What passive aggressive behaviour you use to hurt your ex?	How frequently you engage with it?			Are your children aware of it?	
	Rarely	Some-times	All the time	Yes	No

Anger can be also manifested in many other ways. Completing Table 15.7 will enable you to identify the ways in which you express your anger.

Dr Shlomo Brook

Table 15.7   How Do You Express Your Anger?

How is your anger expressed?	Tick	Example	How frequently do you engage in it?		
			Rarely	Sometimes	All the time
Verbally					
Screaming					
Saying hurtful things					
Swearing					
Threatening					
Making sarcastic remarks					
Sulking					
Other:					
Behaviourally					
Throwing objects					
Breaking things					
Slamming doors					
Doing nothing					
Other:					

Anger has direct and indirect consequences on your relationships with the current important figures in your life. In Table 15.8 you can explore the effects of your anger on the relationships you have.

Table 15.8   How Does Anger Affect Your Relationship With:

Effect of anger on your relationships with...	Explain
Your ex spouse	
Your Family	
Your Children	
Your Co – Workers	
Your friends	
Your neighbours	
Others:	

How Can You Prevent Anger?

Zillman, D. (1979), describes several directives which can help you to cope with your anger and which will foster better interpersonal relationships.

1.   **Re-evaluate your actions:** Re-evaluate your own actions. Maybe

what you say or do sounds hostile to your ex-spouse which might lead to retaliatory behaviour. In other words, be aware of your own provocative anger-provoking behaviour. Remember, your ex-spouse might already be upset and can easily be provoked. Your ex-spouse might wrongly attribute a deliberate, hostile purpose to your actions which will justify retaliation. Your ex-spouse might be prone to accepting and justifying his own angry reaction to your behaviour. It is imperative that you are able to bridge the false perceptive gap in order to prevent a further escalation of anger.

2. **Re-evaluate your spouse's reaction:** Don't take your ex-spouse's behaviour at face value as it might be wrongfully perceived. You need to re-evaluate your ex-spouse's behaviour before you draw any premature conclusions. Each time you make contact with your ex-spouse you must be prepared for the possibility that s/he is as stressed and as vulnerable as you are, and that both of you can be easily provoked. In other words, don't put gasoline on an existing fire.

3. **Reduce any anger-provoking behaviour.** Try to reduce as much as you can any purposeful provocation. If your action is offensive, be ready to apologise and express remorse. Prompt apologies will immediately curtail angry responses. On the other hand, if you possess the "gift" of annoying your ex-spouse unnecessarily, then the best way to de-escalate the situation is to apologise and show regret. Such a functional attitude will abort an explosive situation and will eliminate angry outbursts.

4. **Monitor your spouse's arousal state**: During any interaction with your ex-spouse, be aware of your own, as well as of your ex-spouse's excitement levels. If you judge either of these to be too high, disengage. If you see that your ex-spouse becomes irritable and short-tempered and starts hyperventilating and gets red in the face, don't push your luck, disengage, and let your ex-spouse cool

down before you re-engage.

5. **Be empathic to your ex-spouse's situation:** You need to be aware of the possible difficulties your actions might cause to your ex-spouse. Understanding your ex-spouse's predicament is called empathy. Acknowledging the difficulties your ex-spouse is experiencing will probably reduce his/her bitterness and frustration. Convey your sincere understanding to your ex-spouse. A false acknowledgment of his/her situation might lead to immediate retaliation as this could be viewed as sarcastic and provocative.

6. **Be aware of the presence of a mind-altering or intoxicating state when engaging with your ex-spouse**: Should you suspect your ex is under the influence of alcohol or any other mind-altering drug, be aware that his/her judgement will be severely impaired. Having impaired judgment will affect his/her reasoning and his/her decision-making. Dealing with an intoxicated ex-spouse can be dangerous and requires quick disengagement and a call for help.

As a general rule of thumb, if the conditions for a logical and rational negotiation with your angry ex-spouse are impossible, disengagement will be your best option.

There are several additional ways by which you can reduce your anger. Whenever you become angry just wait, take time out and refrain from action. Although it sounds simple, it is quite an effective way to reduce your anger. According to Tavris, C. (1989) "Any emotional arousal will simmer down if you just wait long enough".

Disengagement serves two purposes. Firstly, it prevents the escalatory process that is a basic feature of any conflict. Secondly, disengaging from your ex will provide you with the distance needed to re-evaluate the situation which might open up new angles and perspectives. In general, whenever your ex-spouse becomes intransigent or quarrelsome it is better for both of you to take time out and to disengage.

In addition, constant rumination on a situation is counter-productive. Moreover, according to Rusting, C. (1998), constant rumination regarding the causes of anger serves to catalyse your anger. Another effective way to eliminate anger which has developed from your tarnished relationship is to communicate your feelings to your ex-spouse in a more assertive manner. Assertive communication of your feelings might foster a better empathic reaction from your ex which, in turn may potentially reduce hostility. In simple terms, it means that if your ex-spouse hurts you or treats you inappropriately let him/her know that you will not tolerate such behaviour. Furthermore, it is important to convey clearly to your ex-spouse that you will not be able to meet all of his/her needs.

In addition, try to use more humour if you can, and you will be surprised to see how effective this can be in scaling down tension.

Get involved in tension-reducing activities such as exercise, yoga, meditation, or listen to relaxing music as this can be very helpful in reducing your anger.

Completing Table 15.9 will help you to identify any potential pleasurable activities that might reduce your anger.

Table 15.9   The Pleasure Activities Log

Date & Time	Scheduled pleasured Activity	Level of pleasure		% of your anger reduction 0%
		Potential 0%	Actual 0%	
		100%	100%	100% less
Sunday				
Monday				
Tuesday				
Wednesday				
Thursday				
Friday				
Saturday				

Use Cognitive Reappraisal of the Divorce Event

Logical re-evaluation of the situation can significantly reduce your anger. As I mentioned earlier, anger is associated with distorted logic and impaired judgment. The greater your anger grows, the more distorted your logic becomes, and the less able you are to appreciate the situation.

Completing Table 15.10 will enable you to re-assess the divorce-related events and the way you judge them. Re-assign an alternative logical and positive explanation to each event and observe how it affects your anger.

Table 15.10   Re-evaluate the Divorce-Related Events:

The situation	Your initial thoughts	Re evaluation of the event from a differ-ent perspec-tive	% change in your anger levels 0%= no change 100%=max. reduction	
			Before	**After**

Increased awareness of your initial reaction to any divorce-related situation might reduce your anger and will hopefully improve communication and future interaction.

Remember, divorce is highly stressful and has a high potential for conflict.

Changing your attitude might have a positive effect on your ex-spouse, and might provide an opportunity to depart from your old familiar dysfunctional hostile interaction and turn it into a positive and productive relationship.

Key Points

- Anger is commonly experienced during the divorce process.
- Anger has cognitive, emotional and physical components.
- Anger has a negative impact on your physical health.
- Cognitive Reappraisal of the divorce-related events can reduce anger.

References and Suggested Readings

1. Zillmann, D. (1988). *The encyclopaedia of mental health.* Academic press.
2. Digiuseppe, R. & Tafrate, R.C. (2007). *Understanding anger disorder.* Oxford: University Press.
3. Averill, J. (1983). Studies on anger and aggression: implications for theories on emotion. *American Psychologist*, 38: 1145-1160.
4. Geen, R.G. (2001). *Human Aggression* (2nd ed.) New York: Open University Press.
5. Bushman, B. J., Baumeiser, R. (1999). Catharsis, Aggression and Persuasive influence: Self fulfilling or self defeating prophecies. *Journal of Personality and Social Psychology,* 76 (3): 367-376.
6. Schwartz, G.E., Weinberger, D. (1981). Cardiovascular differentiation of happiness, sadness, anger and fear following imagery and exercise. *Psychosomatic Medicine*, 43(4): 343-364.

7.   Williams, J.E., Paton, C. (2000). Anger proneness predicts coronary heart disease risk: Prospective analysis from the atherosclerosis risk in the community (ARIC) study. *Circulation,* 101: 2034-2039.

8.   Change, P.P., Ford, D.E (2002). Anger in young men and subsequent premature cardiovascular disease: the precursors study. *Archives of Internal Medicine,* 162: 901-906. (p.439).

9.   Wolf, S., Goodell, H. (1968). *Stress and disease.* Springfield, IL: Charles C Thomas.

10.   Riley, V. (1981). Psychoneuroendocrine influence on immuno – competence and neoplasia. *Science,* 212: 1100-1109.

11.   Zillman, D. (1979). *Hostility and aggression.* Hillsdale, NJ: Erlbaum.

12.   Tavris, C. (1989). *Anger: the misunderstood emotion* (Rev. ed.) New York: Touchstone.

13.   Rusting, C.L. & Nolen-Hoeksema, S. (1998). Regulating responses to anger: Effect of rumination and distraction on angry mood. *Journal of Personality and Social Psychology,* 74: 790-803. (p. 425).

14.   Witvliet, C., Ludwig, T. (2001). Granting forgiveness or harbouring grudges: implications for emotions, physiology and health. *Psychological Science,* 12: 117-123.(p. 425).

15.   Edmund, S. Higgins, M.S.G. (2007). *The neuroscience of clinical psychiatry.* Lippincot: Williams & Wilkins.

SIXTEEN

Guilt in Divorce

"He who can't endure the bad will not live to see the good".
Yiddish proverb

The Purpose

The purpose of this chapter is to explain the guilt you **are** experiencing and its treatment.

Introduction

Guilt is an emotional state which is commonly experienced during the early stages of divorce. Guilt often develops earlier in the case of the divorce initiator and much later in the instance of the person who was dumped.

The amount of guilt you could experience depends on how greatly your actions departed from your values. The further your actions stray from your morals, the greater the chance that you might feel guilty. During the divorce, the Dumper will mainly experience guilt in the early stages of the divorce, while the dumped spouse's guilt feelings will develop at a much later stage.

The decision to get a divorce is often associated with guilt and remorse which is created by the amount of perceived pain inflicted on the nuclear and extended family and friends.

Inflicting pain and suffering on others invariably generates some level of guilt in most people. The bigger the envisaged hurt you cause, the stronger the chance that you are going to feel guilty.

What is Guilt and How is it Formed?

Guilt is an emotional state which develops pursuant to a perceived violation of personal and societal moral rules.

Guilt develops in order to prevent any harmful behaviour which will clash with society's moral rules. In other words, guilt serves as a psychological punishment for any activities which are perceived to be harmful, and in violation of society's moral code.

Shame is a similar emotional reaction to guilt, which is experienced as a result of a similar violation of societal moral rules. Guilt develops early in life by assimilating parental and societal values. In other words, you learn from your parents and other significant figures in your life to distinguish between right and wrong. Choosing to do wrong invariably makes you feel guilty and makes you expect punishment.

Once the assimilation process of societal norms is finished, these remain like an inescapable psychological stick in your head. The punishment for breaking social moral codes is automatic, inescapable and ruthless. In other words, you carry in your head a built-in-stick which takes the form of shame and guilt, and which is activated each time you violate society's values.

The assimilation of social morals never ceases to exist, and is an ongoing active process by which you continue to assimilate additional moral codes as you grow.

Many studies could show that personality disposition to develop guilt is negatively correlated with criminal behaviour. In other words, criminals and antisocial personalities experience very little guilt whenever they violate basic society norms. This is due either to the criminals' innate inability to experience guilt or to their lack of childhood exposure to basic moral values. Antisocial individuals will not experience guilt whenever they break society's values as they don't have the internal psychological stick which called guilt.

On the other side of the spectrum, there are many individuals who have an over-developed conscience which produces super-guilt. In other words, their internal stick is prominent, and becomes overactive even in the face of imagined or perceived violations of basic societal norms.

Such individuals with hypertrophied guilt tend to be socially inhibited and dependent on others. Only those individuals who have the appropriate amount of guilt will be able to conform to society's norms and yet be able to function normally. The various amounts of guilt and its effect on behaviour is illustrated in Figure 16.1.

Figure16.1   Guilt and Behaviour

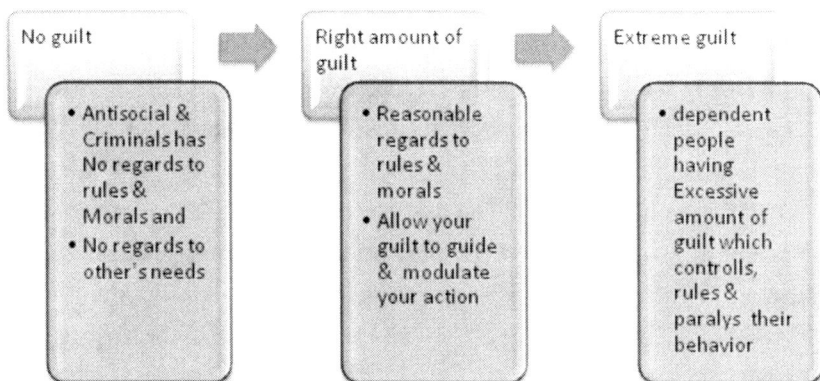

Living in society requires adherence to basic rules which regulate and protect all members of the society. For example, stealing is socially unacceptable, and this is a rule which has to be assimilated at early age. Violation of such a basic rule is a punishable offence. From an early age, a child gets to know this basic rule which is further implemented by the judicial system later in life.

The amount of guilt experienced varies from person to person. Individuals with Antisocial personality disorder do not experience guilt while those individuals with severe depression usually battle with excessive and crippling feelings of guilt.

The amount of guilt experienced relates to the degree to which your actions violate your society's norms. In simple terms, if you do something which is considered to be wrong by your society, then you will probably feel bad.

Therefore it is not surprising to see that people who are going through a divorce have a huge amount of guilt as they often feel that they have let their extended family down.

The divorce initiator is more vulnerable to developing guilt as the decision to move out of the marriage might potentially hurt the family, and will violate the basic foundations of society.

In addition, most religions tend to view marriage as a sacred union sanctioned by God. Getting a divorce will automatically violate religious values which can lead to severe guilt, especially in those individuals who have a strong religious orientation.

Therefore, any act that goes against your personal and societal values, as well as against your religious beliefs will invariably lead to strong feelings of shame and guilt. The amount of guilt will be proportional to the extent by which you have violated your personal and societal values. Therefore, if you consider marriage as sacred and as an important social unit you will most probably feel very bad and guilty about destroying your marriage.

The following vignette further illustrates guilt and its effects on the individual.

Since his departure from home John discovered how difficult single life is. At night he had problems falling asleep, and his mind constantly kept wondering whether his move away from home was the right thing to do. John felt extremely uncomfortable when he had to speak to his estranged wife, and felt increasingly anxious and moody. He was also uncomfortable talking to his family and friends and started to avoid them. He experienced a constant nagging tendency to blame himself for destroying his children's future.

How to Measure Your Guilt?

You can measure your guilt by looking at the various guilt attributes. In general, the stronger your feelings of guilt, the higher the emotional pain you will experience, and the less functional you will become. You will constantly question your actions, and you will always assume the worse. You will feel bad about yourself, and will expect and often welcome punishment that will absolve you and relieve your unpleasant feelings. Completing Table 16.2 will help you measure your social and personal attributes that can cause guilt, while Table 16.3 will measure your current guilt.

Table 16.2   Measure Your Attitude Regarding Marriage and Divorce

How impor-tant is it for you?	Not important at all = 0	Slightly important = 1	Very important = 2
Societal at-tributes			
What people say about you			
What your friends will say			
What your fam-ily will say			
Personal attributes			
To be married			
Being divorced will hurt the people impor-tant to you			
See divorce as a personal failure			
Your religious attributes			
To stay married			
To be divorced			
View divorce as a sin			

Total	
0–6 = weak values regarding marriage & divorce	Marriage is not your cup of tea and getting a divorce is not a big deal for you
7–12 = moderate values regarding divorce	Getting a divorce makes you feel uncomfortable
13–18 = strong values about marriage & divorce	Getting a divorce is a disaster

Table 16.3   Measure Your Guilt

How important is it for you?	Don't mind = 0	Slightly bothered = 1	Feel very concerned = 2
Divorce will hurt your children emotionally			
Divorce will hurt your children financially			
Divorce will hurt your extended family			
Divorce will hurt your religious status			
Divorce will hurt your work status			

Divorce makes you feel bad about yourself			
Divorce makes you uncomfortable interacting with your neighbours			
You are unable to function properly as a result of your actions			
Total			
< 8 Low guilt levels	Despite of the difficulties, you don't feel much guilt and are able to go on with your life.		
9 – 16 High guilt levels	You feel very guilty. It is difficult for you to take proper action. Some of your actions feel as if they are self-punishing.		

In general, guilt is an unpleasant emotional experience and can have a negative impact on your life and on your functioning.

How You can Eliminate Your Guilt?

There are two ways to reduce your guilt.
• Get punishment
• Increase self-awareness regarding personal values and the effects of your actions.

Get Punishment

Guilt is a psychological construct which involves an emotional reaction to "bad" behaviour. However, getting physical punishment instead of emotional punishment might reduce the psychological need to feel guilty.

During the divorce, each side may often engage in self-destructive uncharacteristic behaviour which can be seen as an attempt to reduce each party's guilt.

Examples of punishment-seeking behaviour are the divorced woman who uncharacteristically becomes involved with numerous men whom she has picked up in the local pub and with whom she engages indiscriminately in unprotected sex. Such unusual behaviour might be considered as an attempt to seek punishment and in so doing, to ease the excessive guilt.

Contracting an STD will be regarded, in her subconscious mind, as the most appropriate punishment for the perceived violation of the basic social values.

Engaging in such a punishable behaviour is dangerous, has limited results, and is rarely capable of resolving the amount of guilt. Often, such behaviour will lead to additional guilt and pain.

Another example of guilt-propelled behaviour is the woman who gives up her work, perceived as the cause of the divorce, and spends as much as time as possible with her children in an attempt to relieve her excessive guilt. Once again, the financial hardship that will follow can be seen as a perfect punishment, yet it will result in additional hardships and more pain. Complete Table 16.4 in order to evaluate whether you engage in self-punishing activities.

Table 16.4   Identify Self-Punishing Behaviour

Self-punishing behaviour	Does it make you feel less guilty?		What alternative action should you take?
	Yes Because	No Because	
Example: Left work	*I must have lost my mind. Now I can't afford to pay my bills.*		*Find a new job closer to my children in order to be able to see them more often.*

Increase Awareness Regarding What Makes You Feel Guilty

Understanding what makes you feel guilty and what you can do to change the situation can dramatically affect your guilt.

The ultimate goal is to identify the causes of your guilt and redirect the negative energy into positive behaviour which will lead to growth.

Often, the guilt you experience results from an ill-defined generalised cause. Identifying the correct cause of your guilt will help you to formulate an alternative line of action which will ultimately reduce your guilt.

Completing Table 16.5 will help you to identify the causes responsible for your guilt and enable you to design alternative options that will help you reduce it.

Table 16.5   Who & What Makes You Feel Guilty and How You Can Change it

Who makes you feel guilty?	What make you feel guilty?	How certain are you about the guilt's relevance?		How you can change it
		Little	A lot	
Example: your children who stay with your ex	*Inability to see them regularly*		√	*Phone your children daily and be prepared to take them regularly*

Feeling guilt during divorce is natural. However, whenever it becomes excessive and disabling you need to establish what makes you feel so bad and reduce this to a minimum in order to be able to move on with life.

Key Points

- Guilt is a common emotional state during the divorce.
- Guilt is an emotional state that develops during childhood through the child's interaction with the significant figures in his/her life.
- Guilt serves as an emotional mechanism to direct the child to conform to the social norms and standards.
- Guilt has social, religious and personal attributes.
- Guilt can be reduced either through self-punishing behaviour or by an increased awareness of the causes of the guilt.

Suggested Reading

1. Fisher, B. and Alberti, R. (2000). *Rebuilding, when your relationship ends*. Impact publishers, inc.
2. Weiten, W. (1992). *Psychology themes and variations*. Brooks/Cole publishing company.
3. Comer, R.J. (2007). *Abnormal psychology*. New York: Worth Publishers.

SEVENTEEN

Acceptance, Hope and Forgiveness in Divorce

Yesterday is experience. Tomorrow is hope. Today is getting from one to the other as best as we can".
John M. Henry

The Purpose

The purpose of this chapter is to cover the different aspects of acceptance and hope.

What is Hope ?

Hope is the ability to create a positive expectation of the future. Hope embodies your wish to fulfil your desire to have a positive outcome to your divorce.

During your divorce, you will experience an emotional roller-coaster which includes stress, anxiety, depression and anger. Having all these feelings is common, expected and probably desirable in order to help you to deal with all the issues emanating from your divorce and to be able to resolve them successfully.

However, a successful divorce can be achieved only if you and your ex-spouse as well as your children will be able to work through your emotional reactions and resolve them positively. Only a successful resolution of your emotional responses to the various divorce scenarios will allow you to move on with your life and make the required successful transition to the final emotional stage of divorce, which is the phase of acceptance, hope and forgiveness.

Often, hope is the only beacon that will enable you to navigate the troubled waters of your divorce.

The ability to keep positive hope alive will help you to resolve the ongoing divorce related issues successfully. Keeping positive hope requires you to remember the ultimate goal of a successful divorce, which is to be able to keep a working relationship with your ex while keeping your individuality and your family intact, safe, productive and able to grow.

Losing hope over your ability to have a positive working relationship with your ex–spouse will mean that your goal to have a successful divorce is unattainable. Thus you will view your life as a divorced person to be a failure. Having a negative attitude regarding the outcome of your divorce is demoralising and will sustain your feelings of failure, preventing you from moving forward to build a new life.

On the other hand, having the ability to keep your hope alive, for a better future for yourself and your family, will positively influence your ongoing relationship with your ex-spouse and will enhance your ability to control and to overcome the obstacles ahead.

Hope is mostly a learned experience that you have absorbed from your early interactions with the significant figures in your life. Growing up in a family which displays high levels of abuse, tension and a negative view of life and the future will severely damage your ability to create a hopeful and positive attitude whenever you get exposed to difficult life circumstances.

On the other hand, growing up in a positive and nurturing environment which involves regular encouragement of one's behaviour and instilling hope toward fulfilment of one's potential will foster the development of positive and hopeful thoughts. In simple words, children who are surrounded by a nurturing environment will learn to be more optimistic and more hopeful as grown-ups than those children who grow up in negative and abusive families.

Individuals who resort to more hopeful and positive attitudes also have a more cohesive social support network which they use during difficult periods.

The basic conditions needed to be hopeful are:

- Growing up in a nurturing home.
- Being encouraged to pursue own goals.
- Getting regular and clear messages of belief in their potential and abilities.
- Surrounded by optimistic people.
- Having positive childhood experiences.

Unfortunately, many individuals undergoing divorce did not have the luxury of growing up in a positive and nurturing environment resulting in a reduced ability to develop positive and hopeful thoughts during difficult times. Such individuals tend to resort to more passive behaviour with a negative attitude towards life and the future. They also have a limited ability to create a positive and hopeful vision of their future. Such impaired ability to remain hopeful during difficult times, results in having a more pessimistic, hopeless view of the future which is the hallmark of depression. Table 17.1 will enable you to evaluate your propensity to be hopeful.

Table 17.1   Do You Have a Hopeful Character?

Characteristics	Value score 1......................................10 strongly disagree strongly agree
I set positive life goals	
I never get frustrated	
I always strive to finish what I stated	
I meet the goals that I set	
When I get stuck I look for other possibilities	
I always encourage myself	
I always look at the bright side of events	
I am always hoping for the best	
Pessimism is not in my vocabulary	
It is always important for me to look for a meaning	
Your total score:	
Interpretation	
0 – 33	You are naturally pessimistic and always look at the negative side of the situation
34 – 66	You have a moderate optimistic inclination
67 – 100	You have a strong optimistic inclinations and always try to see the positive side of the situation.

The divorce which you are going through poses a huge challenge to you and to your family. There are multiple issues and problems that need to be resolved. Each solution you make is unique and meaningful to you and has broader consequences on your life and that of your children. Having a pessimistic attitude towards the issues and problems you face every day, will negatively influence your decisions and will ultimately have an adverse impact on your life and on the lives of those around you.

On the other hand, facing your daily problems, from the simplest to the most complex of problems with a hopeful and positive perspective will enhance the possibility of having a more positive outcome.

Having a positive and hopeful attitude will help you to face the challenges your divorce creates and will ultimately result in personal growth, creating the opportunity for a new and more positive beginning. This process is illustrated in figure 17.2:

Figure 17.2   The Effect of Hope and Pessimism on the Outcome of the Divorce Related Issues.

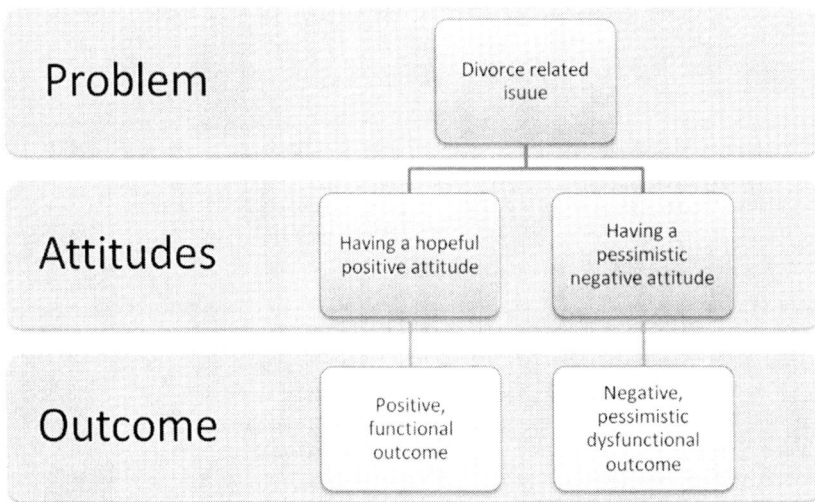

Problem	Divorce related isuue	
Attitudes	Having a hopeful positive attitude	Having a pessimistic negative attitude
Outcome	Positive, functional outcome	Negative, pessimistic dysfunctional outcome

Each issue you are facing during your divorce can be made positive by your ability to assign an optimistic meaning to the given divorce related issue. Your task should be to discover the unique hopeful meaning which each situation has to offer.

There are several ways to enhance your ability to discover the hidden

positive hopeful aspect of the situation.
• Get involved in a creative activity that will enrich your views.
• Get involved in a meaningful and fulfilling activity.
• Get involved with people who will enrich your world.

The first step to learning how to become hopeful and positive is to move away from your passive behaviour by creating a forward motion toward a positive and realistic goal. You have to learn how to create a positive goal and translate it into a positive action; by doing so you will nourish your ability to feel hopeful about yourself and your future. Complete Table 17. 3 in order to gain a better insight into your ability to enhance hopeful attitudes.

Table 17.3   **Creating Positive Goals to Promote Hope**

The goal	Means to achieve it	Timeline	Measuring achievement	Does it make you more hopeful?	
				Yes	No
1 Getting a medical aid	*1 Make appointment with your insurance broker*	*By Friday*	*Signing the contract with the medical aid*		
2					
3					
4					

5					
6					
7					
8					
9					
10					

The goals you set must be self generated which ultimately will serve you in your quest for having a positive and more hopeful future.

The goals you set must be realistic and within your reach. It is nice to have grandiose dreams, but often these are unrealistic and unobtainable. On the other hand, if you are able to create a realistic goal that you can easily achieve and measure, you will be able to enhance your ability to view your life in a more hopeful manner.

Developing and building a hope can be a learned experience. Lacking the ability to think positively due to adverse childhood experiences does not mean that you will never be able to have that skill. You are able to cultivate your ability to be hopeful. Creating positive goals is one way to enhance your positive attitude and hope regarding your current situation. A successful achievement of the goals you have set for yourself can improve your confidence in your abilities to be able to cope better with the challenges that the divorce creates.

Victor Frankle, in his book, "Man's search for meaning", gives a chilling account of life in the Nazi concentration camps. According to Frankle, only those individuals who could maintain hope survived the Nazi concentration camps regardless of the horrors and the inhuman life circumstances they had to endure. On the other hand, all those individuals who gave up hope did not survive and ultimately succumbed to the grim realities of the camp and died.

Hope was the only force that was able to keep them alive and to be able to cope with the extreme hardships and horrors of the Nazi camps. The ability to nurture hope was life saving for the few survivors who managed to get out alive from the concentration camps. In addition, their ability to keep hope alive was the basic platform with which those survivors were able to build a new life. Although it seems ridiculous to equate divorce to the experiences of those in the Nazi concentration camps, the point is that every difficult situation can be manageable and overcome by keeping a positive attitude and nurturing hope.

In addition to being hopeful, a positive resolution of your divorce requires you to learn how to forgive your ex-spouse and yourself and to be able to accept the past while moving forward with your life.

According to Charlotte Witvliet, forgiveness reduces anger. In her study on college students who practice forgiveness, Charlotte Witvliet was able to demonstrate a reduction in those students' blood pressure, heart rate and perspiration in comparison to their counterparts who were unforgiving and maintained grudges.

Forgiveness is a personal choice that you can make by letting go of the past wrongs made by yourself and your ex-spouse. Being able to forgive your ex–spouse and yourself reflects your personal strength and your desire to grow out of the situation as opposed to weakness and stagnation which accompanies the inability to forgive and accept the past. Being able to forgive and accept the new reality of your divorce will empower you and make you a stronger, healthier and better person.

The ability to forgive will release you from the poisonous effects of hatred and revenge which often accompanies divorce. Your ability to let go of the past means being able to accept the end of your marriage and the ability to put all the past differences behind you which will make you ready to build a new life for yourself and your family.

References

1. Witvliet, C. Ludwig, T. (2001). Granting forgiveness or harbouring grudges: implications for emotions, physiology and health. Psychological Science, 12, 117-123.(p. 425).
2. Frankle, V.E. (1962). Man's search for meaning, an introduction to logotherapy, New York: A Touchstone Book.

CPSIA information can be obtained at www.ICGtesting.com
Printed in the USA
BVOW032207280612

293975BV00006B/5/P